The Ten Skills of
Highly Effective People

THE TEN SKILLS OF HIGHLY EFFECTIVE PEOPLE

Samuel A. Malone

The Liffey Press

Published by
The Liffey Press Ltd
Ashbrook House, 10 Main Street
Raheny, Dublin 5, Ireland

A catalogue record of this book is
available from the British Library.

ISBN 1-904148-95-6

Printed in Ireland by ColourBooks Ltd.

CONTENTS

Preface ix

THE TEN SKILLS OF HIGHLY EFFECTIVE PEOPLE
(THE OPTIMISTIC MODEL) 1

1. OBJECTIVES 2
Importance of Goals 4
Stretch Goals 5
SMARTS 7
Why People Don't Set Goals 8
Types of Goals 11
The Need for Multiple Goals 13
Basic Questions for Goals 14
Different Strokes for Different Folks 15
Purpose, Goals and Greatness 17
Summary 18
Five Steps to Setting Better Objectives 18
Case Study 19
Mind Map of Chapter 21

2. PLANS 22
Importance of Planning 24
What Does Planning Involve? 24
The ASPIRE Model 25
Barriers to Planning 27
A Planned Approach to Work 28
Personal Development Plans 29
Summary 30
Five Steps to Making Better Plans 31
Case Study 31
Mind Map of Chapter 33

3. TENACITY **34**
Commitment 36
Persistence 37
Patience 40
Most Quitters Fail 41
Resolutions 42
Resilience 43
Stamina 48
Summary 49
Five Steps to Improving Your Tenacity 50
Case Study 50
Mind Map of Chapter 53

4. INTEGRITY **54**
Personal Code of Ethics 55
Character 56
A Sense of Values 57
The Character Creed 60
Lies and Deceit 61
Trust 63
Summary 64
Five Steps to Improving Your Integrity 65
Case Study 65
Mind Map of Chapter 67

5. MOTIVATION **68**
Source 70
Unique Drivers 71
Hope 72
Expectation 75
The Pygmalion Effect 76
The Placebo Effect 77
Passion 78
How to Motivate Yourself 80
Summary 83
Five Steps to Improving Your Motivation 84
Case Study 84
Mind Map of Chapter 87

6. INTERPERSONAL RELATIONSHIPS **88**
Popular People.. 90
IQ + EQ = Success... 91
Communication Skills 93
Listening 94
Making an Impression.. 96
Assertiveness... 98
My Bill of Rights 99
Basic Assertiveness Skills 100
Shy People 102
Overcoming Shyness 102
Summary 105
Five Steps to Improving Interpersonal Relationships 106
Case Study 106
Mind Map of Chapter 109

7. SELF-ESTEEM **110**
High Self-esteem.. 112
Exercise and Self-esteem.. 114
Self-talk 115
Personal Development and Self-esteem 116
Self-worth... 117
Self-efficacy 117
Learned Helplessness 119
Limits of Self-esteem 120
Narcissism... 120
Dark Side of High Self-esteem 121
Low Self-esteem.. 124
Self-sabotage 125
How to Raise Your Self-esteem... 127
Summary 129
Five Steps to Improving Your Self-esteem............................. 130
Case Study 130
Mind Map of Chapter 133

8. THINKING POSITIVELY **134**
Positive Thinking 136
Optimists... 137
Pessimists.. 139

Poor Thinking Habits 142
Happiness 145
How to be Happy 150
ABCDE Technique 155
Summary 157
Five Steps to Improving Positive Thinking 158
Case Study 158
Mind Map of Chapter 161

9. IMPROVEMENT 162
Change 164
Lifelong Learning 166
The Brain and Learning 167
Multiple Intelligence 169
Learning Effectively 171
Making the Most of Your Memory 172
Ageing and the Brain 173
The Flow Zone 176
Summary 177
Five Steps Towards Personal Improvement 178
Case Study 179
Mind Map of Chapter 181

10. CONTROL 182
Self-discipline 184
Work-Life Balance 186
Locus of Control 187
The Comfort Zone 189
Control Your Time 192
Control Your Money 195
Summary 196
Five Steps to Improve Control 198
Case Study 198
Mind Map of Chapter 201

References and Bibliography 203
Index 207
About the Author 211

PREFACE

This book is about how to lead a successful and fulfilling life. Success doesn't necessarily mean fabulous riches or fame. It means leading a purposeful, happy and contented life with adequate financial means to do whatever you desire. The book is organised around the acronym *OPTIMISTIC*. This acronym will help you to memorise and recall the skills you need to grow and develop and realise your dreams. The skills are soundly backed up by the best psychological research currently available. Each letter stands for a particular skill:

- **O**bjectives. These will provide the purpose and goals and give a guiding and controlling force to reach your targets. A rudderless ship will not get to its destination and will finish up stranded on the shore or destroyed on the rocks. Similarly a person without a vision, mission and objectives will be without direction and fall prey to the temptations and vicissitudes of life. Research consistently shows that people with goals in life are more successful than people without goals.

- **P**lans. Objectives and plans are dependent and interconnected. Plans must be implemented to achieve your objectives. Actions such as strategies and tactics are required to turn objectives into reality. Nothing gets done until you actually do something.

- **T**enacity. Determination, perseverance and patience are what get you there in the end. As you go through life you will meet setbacks, obstacles, traumatic events and failures on the way. These should be seen as challenges to be over-come and learning opportunities on the journey to the successful attainment of your objectives.

- **I**ntegrity. This is the old-fashioned concept of having a good character. Being honest, genuine, truthful, fair and reliable are some of the traits needed for a successful and happy life. Like business, personal relationships are built on trust. Trust is the foundation for successful relationships.

- **M**otivation. This is the driving force that propels you towards your goals. There are two basic types of motivation: intrinsic and extrinsic. Intrinsic comes from within yourself and is considered the most compelling force to drive you forward towards the achievement of your targets. There is no substitute in life for inherent interest, sense of vocation, enthusiasm, passion and hope. However, extrinsic motivators such as praise and encouragement will also facilitate the process.

- **I**nterpersonal relationships. In life we need to network, influence others and get their support to achieve our goals. Developing self-awareness, empathy, communication and assertiveness skills will help you realise your ambitions. Getting along with others is an essential skill if you want to live a happy and successful life. Overcoming shyness will help you improve your relationships with others.

- **S**elf-esteem. You must love and respect yourself if you expect others to do likewise. High self-esteem is crucial to our well-being and self-development. People with high self-esteem see threats as opportunities and weaknesses as projects for improvement. People with low self-esteem lack confidence, fail to exploit their natural talents and abilities and thus never reach their true potential. To be successful in life we must see ourselves as worthwhile, capable and effective.

- **T**hinking positively. Optimistic people tend to be healthier, happier and more successful socially, academically and in their careers than pessimistic people. Optimists look at the past with satisfaction, live in the present with purpose and look to the future with optimism and hope. You can take practical steps to improve your happiness.

- **I**mprovement. Just like a business we need to continually improve and develop ourselves if we want to be successful throughout our life and career. The days of throwing away the books after leaving college are gone. Knowledge is now out of date within five years and so there is a need for continuous updating of existing knowledge and development of new knowledge and skills.

- **C**ontrol. People go off the rails because they lose control of their lives. Self-discipline, emotional intelligence, combining the work ethic with work-life balance, financial acumen and time management are some of the skills needed to put you on track and keep you there.

I recommend that you memorise the *OPTIMISTIC* acronym. Write it out on a 5 x 3 card. Bring the card around with you for a few days and repeat it until it goes into your long-term memory. You now have absorbed into your unconscious mind the 10 skills of highly successful people. Put them into practice in your everyday life and judge the results for yourself. Tackle one at a time. You will need to continually practise the ten skills throughout your life. Remember, this is a life-long project rather than a one-day wonder. Success requires long-term commitment backed up by short-term action plans.

There are ten chapters in the book, each one devoted to a particular skill. To facilitate the learning process each chapter is preceded by an overview diagram called the "Success Wheel", and concludes with a summary, a five-step plan for improving that particular skill, a case study and a mind map™. To reinforce the learning and memorisation process and bring the principles alive, practical advice, inspirational stories and quotations, and acronyms are interspersed throughout each chapter. It is suggested that you read the summary and study the mind map for each chapter before you read it in detail. This will give you a framework to "hook" the information on and help you remember it better. No matter what stage of life you're at you will find this book an inspirational read. It is packed with very useful and practical advice to help you on your journey through a successful life.

Tony Buzan is the creator of Mind Maps™. The term "Mind Maps™" is the registered trademark of Tony Buzan. Many thanks to David Givens, publisher and Brian Langan, editor, of The Liffey Press, who shaped and fine-tuned the manuscript into its present attractive format.

Good luck in your efforts to become a more successful person!

Samuel A. Malone
March 2006

THE TEN SKILLS OF HIGHLY SUCCESSFUL PEOPLE

(THE OPTIMISTIC MODEL)

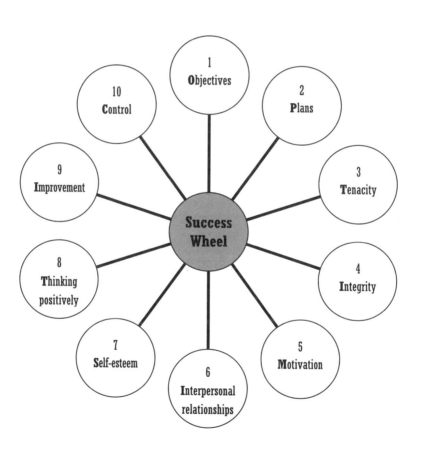

1

OBJECTIVES

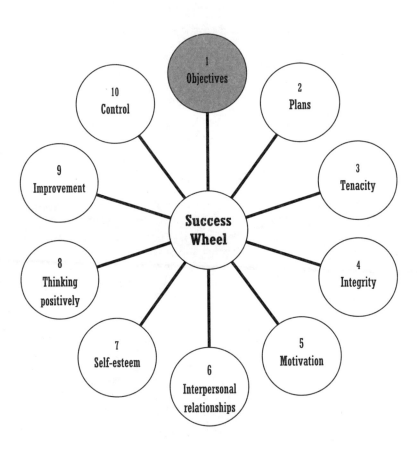

* Why are objectives important?
* What are the SMARTS for objectives?
* Why do most people fail to make objectives?
* What is the difference between a vision, mission and objective?

> **"Anyone who consciously becomes a goal setter, writes them down, and frequently thinks and talks about them will notice an immediate and dramatic improvement in their level of accomplishment, even if they've done very little with their lives before." — Brian Tracey**

O stands for objectives and is the first letter of our acronym OPTIMISTIC. As far as this chapter is concerned the terms objectives and goals are used interchangeably. An objective is a specific, realistic and measurable aim to be achieved within a time and cost constraint. Research confirms that people who make objectives are more successful than people who fail to do so. Objectives should focus on a vision and mission. Objectives provide a source of motivation and a sense of purpose and direction for those who want to achieve things in life. Objectives should be specific, measurable, achievable, relevant, timely and supported (SMARTS). There are all sorts of reasons why people don't set goals including procrastination and fear of failure.

Importance of Goals

Goals will give you a reason to get up in the morning with a burning desire to do the things you need to do. Goals help you keep your eye on the ball, serve as a monitoring device to assess progress and identify and deal with the obstacles that may prevent you from achieving them. Obstacles might include lack of commitment, money and time resources and should be viewed as challenges to be overcome and opportunities to learn.

> **"Crystallise your goals. Make a plan for achieving them and set yourself a deadline. Then, with supreme confidence, determination and disregard for obstacles and other people's criticisms, carry out your plan." — Paul J. Meyer**

Goals provide you with positive self-direction, intensity and duration of action. They provide purpose and focus which means you live by design rather than default. Having goals will direct your attention, time, energy, talents and skills to where they are most needed and effective. The brain is a goal seeking mechanism. This means that whatever goal you implant on your subconscious it will continuously work to achieve it. Michael J. Gelb, author of *How to Think Like Leonardo da Vinci,* said: "Brain researchers estimate that your unconscious data base outweighs the conscious on an order exceeding ten million to one. This database is the source of your hidden, natural genius. In other words, a part of you is much smarter than you are. The wise people regularly consult that smarter part."

The subconscious abhors a vacuum and will not rest until it attracts the people and resources needed to accomplish your goals. Goals ensure that you are proactive rather than reactive. Setting goals means that you are taking responsibility for your own life rather than being subject to the whim of others. Many people live aimless lives at the mercy of chance preferring to do without the discipline of having goals.

People are happiest when pursuing worthwhile goals. You are responsible for setting the goals and achieving the targets set. As you sow, so shall you reap. The old saying, "If it's going to be, it's up to me" is also appropriate in this context. Goals provide the focus for the organisation of time, energy and resources, both physical and mental. Success is a progressive realisation of goals.

Written Goals Are Best

A Harvard University study on goals in 1953 showed that people who set written goals were more successful, happier and more fulfilled in their lives than their contemporaries. In this study only three per cent of a graduating class were found to have set written goals together with a plan for achieving them. Twenty years later the three per cent had accomplished more in their lives than the other 93 per cent combined. Subsequent studies have confirmed these findings.

Write down your major goals on a card and carry them around with you. Continuously review your goals each day so that they become imprinted on your mind. This will remind you of the actions you must take to bring your goals to fruition. What's impressed on your subconscious mind will be expressed in your actions. Update your goals over time in line with your changing priorities, resources and life circumstances.

Achieving goals will make you a better person than you were previously. You will grow in the process gaining knowledge and expertise that nobody can take away from you. Wealth, power, and fame can be taken away but what you have learnt and become in the process of achieving your goals can never be taken from you. You have become a different person with different skills and attitudes and new capabilities.

Stretch Goals

Goals should stretch your capabilities and provide you with a challenge. In other words, they should be manageable but difficult. They should be tough but realistic and attainable. Goals that are too easy to achieve create boredom. Goals that are too difficult to achieve may lead to feelings of failure, anxiety and undermine morale. People committed to a goal will exert effort in proportion to what it takes to achieve the goal. So an easy goal will stimulate low effort, a medium goal moderate effort and a difficult goal high effort.

Stretch goals should be compatible with your self-image, needs, values, talents, interests and lifestyle preference and provide the necessary spurt to growth and development. People's priorities change over a lifetime; therefore goals should also be formulated in such a way that they can be adapted to changing circumstances. Goals in harmony with your values and self-image are more likely to be inspirational. For example, a person who values education has more reason to pursue a degree to reach their goal. A person who values health has more reason to eat, diet and exercise wisely in order to remain healthy.

"In the absence of clearly-defined goals, we become strangely loyal to performing daily trivia until ultimately we become enslaved by it." — Robert Heinlein

---

The goals selected should be of personal high importance. Stretch goals can dramatically improve your personal productivity and efficiency. They force you to think outside the box and think up creative ways of achieving your aims. In some instances you may have to develop new competencies to achieve your goals. Stretch goals will have a positive impact on your growth and development. The risk/reward trade-off should be appraised so that the implications of failure are considered.

Goals will help you live productively, build necessary competencies and provide motivation to realise your dreams. Goals provide a control mechanism. Targets are set, progress is monitored and corrective action taken as needed. It may be necessary to chunk your goals into sub-goals. Divide and conquer should be your motto. Small steps are easier to accomplish than larger ones. Life is hard by the yard, but by the inch it's a cinch.

SMARTS

This is a well-known acronym for remembering the essential elements of effective goals. It stands for:

- **S**pecific. Goals should be vivid, clear, concrete and crystallised in writing. Specify the goals in a way that you find compelling. Asking someone to "do their best" on a task is too vague. Similarly asking a salesperson to increase sales is not specific enough. This could mean 1 per cent, 2 per cent or any increase. Vague goals will only produce vague results. Unwritten goals are like seeds without soil. Some authorities maintain that goals written down are 20 times more likely to be achieved than goals not made explicit. Use your creative imagination to visualise where you want to be and mentally rehearse the steps you must take to get you there.

- **M**easurable. What can't be measured is rarely done. If you can't measure it, you can't manage it. Have regard to quality, quantity, time and cost. These factors will act as benchmarks and help you plan and control your activities. They will also indicate when your goal has been achieved. In the meantime, corrective action may be needed to bridge the gap between the desired and actual situation and put you back on target again.

- **A**chievable. Objectives should be reasonable and capable of achievement. You must believe that you can achieve or make progress towards a goal because it is hard to be motivated by something that you perceive as being unattainable. If I have high self-efficacy I will set difficult but achievable goals. However, don't set yourself up for failure by setting unrealistic goals. The more realistic and attainable your goals the more likely you are to succeed and feel good about yourself when you do. Have confidence in your ability to solve problems and overcome obstacles on the journey to your goals. On the other hand, if your self-efficacy is low you will reflect on your inadequacies and thereby undermine your ability to achieve your goals.

- **R**elevant. Objectives should be relevant and pertinent to your interests. Objectives created by you rather than somebody else will have your sincere commitment, as they are inherently motivational. You know you have the right goals when they move, inspire and incite you to action. The right goals will be congruent with your self-image and thus in harmony with your values.

- **T**imely. Goals should be time-bound. That which can be done at any time is rarely ever done. Time constraints concentrate the mind and create a sense of urgency. Deadlines and time schedules create a challenge and focus your energies on the achievement of completion times.

- **S**upported. State the resources — physical, financial and mental — needed to achieve your goals. Decide who, how, when and where you will need support to help you achieve your objectives. It is a good idea to let your friends and colleagues know what you are trying to achieve and how they can be of assistance to you. Seek out a coach or mentor to help you achieve your goals. It takes courage to seek out help when you need it. Consider any additional training that you may need to support your aims.

Why People Don't Set Goals

In practice most people shy away from setting goals. Some experts estimate that up to 95 per cent of people do not set goals. The 5 per cent who do set goals control the rest of us who don't. In addition, those who do set goals rarely put them in writing. Some of the reasons why people don't set goals include:

- **Fear of failure**. Fear of failure leads to indecision which in turn leads to further self-doubt. Most people fail not because they lack the skills or aptitude to achieve their desires but because they lack the self-belief that they can do it. They fear that things will go wrong, that they will not achieve their goals, some disaster will happen and that they will finish up bankrupt. Negative thoughts paralyse them from taking action. Not trying is in fact the ultimate failure. If you're not in, you can't win! Most people regret the things they didn't do rather than the things they tried but failed at. Remember, for every failure there is an alternative course of action. For every obstacles on your road to success there is an alternative route. There are many different ways of achieving your goals. Fear of failure was not a consideration for Leonardo da Vinci, probably one of the greatest inventive geniuses of all time. During his lifetime he developed an innate understanding of optics but lacked the mathematics to grasp the properties of light. He conceived flying devices and tanks but couldn't realise his dreams because the technology of the time was too unsophisticated to build such machines. He left behind him numerous unfinished paintings and incomplete insights.

"The only failure one should fear, is not hugging to the purpose they see as best." — George Eliot

---

- **Fear of ridicule**. Some people fear ridicule, humiliation, criticism and losing face in the event of not achieving their objectives. They thus lack the courage, conviction and willpower to commit their goals to paper and declare their intentions in public. Many famous people were initially ridiculed but nevertheless went on to achieve great success. For example, Marconi, the Italian inventor of the radio, was laughed at when he said he would transmit sound without using wires. In 1909 he received the Nobel Prize for physics. During World War I he developed short-wave radio. He sent the first radio message from Britain to Australia in 1918. Similarly, Brunel, a British engineer, was thought to be silly for thinking that iron ships could float. He proved his detractors wrong when in 1843 he went on to design the first ship with an iron hull and a screw propeller. Fear of ridicule prevents many people from taking risks, pursuing their dreams and achieving great success.

- **Fear of success**. Some people even have a fear of success. They may fear the extra responsibility that success may bring. They don't want to stand out from the crowd and move out of their comfort zone. Peer pressure may hold them back. They may fear that they won't be able to live up to the higher expectations that success may bring. In addition, on successful accomplishment of their goals they may feel guilty and unworthy and may even fear losing their friends. If you lose friends through jealousy, then they were not true friends in the first place. We should realise that after our hard work and commitment we are entitled to all the success we achieve.

- **Procrastination**. This is putting off until tomorrow what you should do today. People keep postponing setting their objectives with the excuse that they are too time-consuming and cumbersome to draw up. Some people confuse intention with action and thus never get around to take the appropriate steps needed to formulate their objectives in writing. What is the first step you need to take to start the process of achieving your goal?

"Many people die with their music still in them. Why is this so? Too often it is because they are always getting ready to live. Before they know it, time runs out." — Oliver Wendell Holmes

---

- **Belief**. They have a negative belief about goals. They are not convinced about the importance of goals and don't understand the crucial role they play in personal and professional success.

- **Don't know how to set precise goals**. They lack the technical skills necessary to clearly formulate their goals in writing. The SMARTS acronym discussed previously will help you formulate meaningful goals.

- **Risk averse**. Setting goals involves risk. There are no rewards without risk. To achieve your goals you may have to change your current lifestyle, adopt new attitudes, work hard, develop new competencies and accept new challenges. All of this means moving outside your comfort zone and doing things you never did before. If you keep on doing the same thing you'll get the same results. To get different results you need to do something different.

- **They confuse desires with goals**. Goals develop from ideas, wants, needs and desires. However, desires need to be transformed into a goal statement that leads to the achievement of the goal itself. For example, a person may desire to be an accountant but to achieve that goal they need to translate it into a specific goal statement like, "I will enrol in a five-year professional accountancy degree programme on 19 September in the local third-level business college. I will register as a student with the relevant professional accountancy body and I will purchase the relevant texts for the first-year examination course. I will draw up a timetable for study".

Types of Goals

Mission, vision and goals are often considered in that order. The mission is your general objective, purpose or vocation in life. It should answer the question "Why am I here?" Without a purpose your life is empty. Some people, such as Mother Teresa, dedicated their lives to people in grave need. Fulfilled human beings dedicate their life to something. For example, an entertainer's mission might be to make people happy. A fashion designer's mission might be to design beautiful clothes and enhance people's self-esteem. The shorter the mission statement the better, as it is easier to remember. Write down your mission on a piece of paper and pin it to the wall where you will see it every day.

"Life means to have something definite to do – a mission to fulfil – and in the measure in which we avoid something, we make it empty. Human life, by its very nature, has to be dedicated to something". — Jose Ortega y Gasset

The subconscious mind can't tell the difference between a real event and one that is vividly imagined. That's why it's so important to visualise the future you want in your mind's eye. What you see is what you eventually get, provided it's more than just wishful thinking and you take the practical steps to make it happen. The vision describes in detail what your destination will look like, feel like, sound like and taste like. A compelling vision will act like a magnet drawing you forcefully to a successful conclusion.

A characteristic of many geniuses is the ability to visualise. In fact, people like Albert Einstein, Leonardo da Vinci, Walt Disney and Wolfgang Amadeus Mozart all ascribed their creative genius to their ability to visualise. Einstein maintained that imagination was more important than knowledge. Bertrand Russell said, "It is only through imagination that men become aware of what the world might be". Sports psychologists now use mental imagery or visualisation to improve athletic performances by getting athletes to set and mentally rehearse the accomplishment of desired outcomes. This performance enhancement technique can be equally effective in management and personal development.

"Setting goals is the first step in turning the invisible into the visible." — Tony Robbins

---

A vision is an inspirational and motivational image of the future you strongly desire. It is unique to you. The vision provides a starting point and anchor for what we do. It should be strong enough to engage your heart and mind. As George Bernard Shaw said, "You see things; and you say, 'why?' But I dream things that never were; and I say 'why not?'" A vision engages the imagination to create dreams and visualise outcomes. As the old adage goes "energy flows where attention goes". The vision translates the mission into images strong enough to focus your attention on. It provides direction and stimulates success. A vision helps you to plan efficiently for the future to accomplish your goals. A vision should be relatively timeless. Goals, on the other hand, must remain flexible enough to achieve the vision.

The Need for Multiple Goals

The mission and vision is the desired end, while goals and action plans are the means of achieving them. Goals are more specific and are capable of measurement. Goals can be long-term, medium-term, short-term and immediate and are ultimately supported by schedules and daily tasks. Goals can be drawn up in relation to different aspects of our lives. We may have goals for health, wealth, career, relationships, learning and even spiritual matters. In turn these goals can be broken down into sub-goals. For example, you might have sub-goals for exercise, nutrition and relaxation to support your health goal. In fact you will need to prioritise those goals you wish to concentrate on.

Most people have multiple goals. We want to be well-educated, healthy, make friends, take exercise, have good careers, pursue lifelong learning and lead happy and fulfilling lives. Setting priorities in goals is critical to a successful life in the short term and long term. It can be dangerous to allow one goal to define your life. Katz et al. (1992) found that it is counterproductive to have a narrow focus and a singular goal. Among the abundance of research that supports this position is the Grant study. This tracked a group of Harvard graduates for more than 50 years. Those with the most successful careers were not necessarily academic superstars, and their professional ambitions have not wholly defined their lives since. Instead, they've allowed themselves to build strong, stable marriages and deep friendships. They've made room in their lives for exercise, relaxation, and multiple interests and activities. They've become best-selling authors, cabinet members, scholars, physicians, judges and captains of industry. They've shown an abundance of initiative rather than blinding ambition. Initiative tends to enliven and open us up to new ideas and opportunities, while ambition tends to enclose us.

Basic Questions for Goals

The following are some critical questions you need to ask your-self when drawing up your mission, vision and goals:

- Who am I? What really matters to me? What are my core values? What am I good at? What do I really enjoy doing? What are the things that make me feel most alive? What do I want to accomplish in life? Considering your childhood dreams might give a clue as to what you really would like to do with your life.

- What do I want out of life? Our most basic goal is to live and be happy. Happiness is about giving and making a contri-bution to others. The possession of power, money and mate-rial things doesn't necessarily bring happiness.

- Where are you now? Take a personal inventory of your re-sources. Resources include abilities, talents, education, ex-perience, time and money. Keep in mind that talent is only converted into a skill by working hard on it.

- Where do you want to be in one year, five years or ten years?

- How can you get there? Is what you are currently doing moving you towards your goals? What do you need to do to bridge the gap between where you are now and where you want to be? For example, a gap analysis may show you need to acquire more resources and develop further competen-cies if you are to realise your goals.

"Our goals can only be reached through a vehicle of a plan, in which we must fervently believe, and upon which we must vigorously act. There is no other route to success." — Pablo Picasso

---

- How will you know when you arrive? What job, income, house, car and lifestyle will you have? Ongoing feedback on performance is essential. You will need to have standards to measure how successful you are in achieving your goals;

otherwise you will have no motivation to take corrective action, change direction or level of effort.

- What did you always want to do but fear to do? Feel the fear and do it anyway. What would you do if you knew you could not fail? If a genie granted you three wishes, what would they be? What would you do if you only had six months to live? The answer to these questions will show what your real priorities and goals in life should be.

Different Strokes for Different Folks

The following scenarios illustrate the type of unique problems people may experience when setting career goals:

Scenario 1

John did a BA in management. He is 24 and has been working as a trainee manager for the past two years with a large retail organisation in the grocery business. After leaving college he rushed into the job without much thought because the money on offer was attractive and he was unsure of what he really wanted. At that stage of life his main priority was to earn money quickly, have a good time and support himself. However, two years on John is unsure about his job choice and is concerned about the future direction of his life and career. He has started to do research about various occupations and industries and has asked his friends and family for advice. Next week he has a meeting with the personnel officer about the different self-assessment instruments available to determine what his aptitudes and interests are and what would be the most suitable career path for him to follow. Although John is undecided about what he really wants to do and thus doesn't have a clear career goal, at least he is actively gathering information about different career opportunities.

Scenario 2

Joan's career has been aimless for many years. At 34 she has had a variety of different jobs over the past 16 years since completing her leaving certificate with four honours and three passes. She finds jobs interesting for a while but then tends to get bored and wants to move on. She currently has a job as a customer representative handling customer problems and complaints. She is not happy with her current job and finds listening to customer complaints stressful. Joan has never set career goals for herself and wouldn't know how to go about it. She lives in the present, tends to be reactive rather than proactive and finds it hard to make decisions and commit to long-term objectives. Joan feels because of her age that starting out on a new career is not a realistic option. Joan is very indecisive and shows a persistent inability to set career goals and think about the direction her career should be going in.

Scenario 3

Bill has an MBA from a good university. He is very ambitious and has set himself clear career goals for moving up the corporate hierarchy. He was introduced to the concept of Management by Objectives during the MBA programme and has transferred the concept to his own life. He has done well in line with his expectations and now holds down a senior management position. He feels that he must work long hours if he is to progress further up the management hierarchy. His workaholic lifestyle has not been without problems. His job entails trips to overseas subsidiaries and he is often away for long periods of time. His wife complains that he is never at home, has no time for his family and has threatened to divorce him. Bill would love to spend more time with his wife and children and envies other fathers who manage to do so. He now realises that his work lifestyle is not consistent with his self-image, values and preferred lifestyle. While Bill has set career goals for himself he has failed to take into account the implications these are having on his personal life.

As these scenarios demonstrate, career goals are necessary for success in life and must be related to the unique circumstances, talents and life-stage of a particular individual. Goals must be compatible with a person's self-image, values, interests, aptitudes and preferred lifestyles. People must have sufficient information to make well-informed decisions before they decide on their career goals.

Purpose, Goals and Greatness

Explorers, inventors, scientists, politicians, writers, composers and artists are all driven by goals. Vision, mission and goals provided the direction, inspiration and motivation for the perseverance and hard work needed to realise their dreams. We should use these people as models to help us achieve our goals.

- Robert E. Peary doggedly pursued his dream for 23 years to reach the North Pole before eventually succeeding on 6 April 1909 after seven failed attempts. Together with his assistant and four Inuit men he became the first person to reach the North Pole and thus assured his place in history.

- Marie Curie spent her entire adult life conducting scientific experiments. She discovered the elements radium and polonium and laid the groundwork for nuclear physics and theories of radioactivity. In 1911 she was awarded a second Nobel prize being the first person to be awarded the Nobel prize twice. She was the most celebrated scientist of her time during a period when science was almost exclusively male dominated.

"The greatest danger for most of us lies not in setting our aim too high and falling short, but in setting our aim too low, and achieving our mark." — Michelangelo

---

- Michelangelo told his father that he wanted to be a great artist. His father wasn't too impressed with the idea but nevertheless Michelangelo went on to become one of Italy's most famous artists and sculptors. His paintings adorn the Sistine Chapel in the Vatican and one of his most famous sculptures is the statue of David. Michelangelo certainly believed in walking the talk and aiming high.

- When Noah Webster was 43, he set himself the goal of writing the first American dictionary of the English language. It took him over 27 years to write his book. When finished in 1828, at the age of 70, Noah's dictionary had 70,000 words in it and became an American classic.

Summary

Research shows that those who set goals are more successful than those who don't. Goals give you a sense of direction and purpose and mean that you are not living at the mercy of chance. Written goals are the most effective. Even chance favours the prepared mind. You must know what you're looking for to exploit the chance opportunity that may come your way.

SMARTS is a well-known acronym for remembering the essential elements of goals. It stands for specific, measurable, achievable, relevant, timely and supported. Following the SMARTS model means that your goals are more likely to be successfully completed.

People fail to set goals because of fear, procrastination and lack of belief. A mission and a vision should precede goals. There are many types of goals including long term, medium term and short term. Goals should be compatible with self-image, values, interests, aptitudes and lifestyle preferences.

Explorers, inventors, scientists, politicians, writers, composers and artists are all driven by visions supported by goals and we should use them as models and sources of inspiration for our own goals.

FIVE STEPS TO SETTING BETTER OBJECTIVES

1. **Write down two reasons why goals are important to you.**

2. **Compose your mission statement and pin it to the wall where you can see it and reflect on it every day.**

3. **Follow the SMARTS acronym when you are writing down your goals. Make sure they are challenging. Record them on cards and review them each day.**

4. **Consider why most people don't set goals. Reflect on these and resolve that they won't ever apply to you.**

5. **Visualise in your mind what you will see, hear and feel when you eventually achieve your goals.**

Case Study: Objectives + Hard Work = Success

Brian worked in an administrative role in a large retail organisation. He left school at 18 with a good leaving certificate (doing particularly well in accountancy) and went to work straight away. He always had an aptitude for figures and had ambitions to be an accountant but financial circumstances at home meant he couldn't afford to go to college and had to pay his way and contribute to the family budget. After four years in his present role Brian got very dissatisfied with his lack of progress in his company. Each year since leaving school he had considered the possibility of studying to be an accountant but kept putting it off for one reason or another. Around this time, Brian attended an in-company course on personal development. Part of the programme dealt with the importance of having a sense of purpose supported by written goals. Brian now realises that he had been drifting aimlessly through life hoping that things would get better and others would lead the way but of course they didn't. He now knows that if things are to change he must change them himself.

Brian inquired from one of the professional accountancy bodies about their qualification and how to go about qualifying. As a non-graduate entrant he would take about five years to qualify provided he passed each exam each year and put in the recommended hours study each week. He knows that the local college provides classes three nights each week between September and April for those preparing for the professional accountancy body he intends to do. This amounts to a total classroom time of nine hours. Another three hours would be used up in commuting time to and from the college. He realises this is a huge time commitment in addition to holding down a full-time job. Most nights and weekend days would have to be devoted to study if he were to achieve his objective of qualifying as an accountant in five years. He now realises that it isn't sufficient just to desire to be an accountant. This desire must be transformed into a written goal statement and action plan to achieve his goal of qualifying.

Brian decided to take up the challenge. Brian set himself the goal of completing his accountancy exams in five years. On the journey to his long-term goal he has set himself the yearly goal of completing each stage of the exams. To formalise the process he drew up a study schedule and timetable setting out the number of hours he must study each week to achieve his yearly goal. Each study session was for one hour and he drew up learning objectives for each session. These kept his mind focused on what he needed to learn during the study session. After each study session he took a small break before starting another. Throughout the academic year he sat "mock" exams to ascertain his progress and to make sure he was getting sufficient exam practice. The ongoing feedback received from these exams was a great source of information to him on what he needed to do to bring his actual progress up to examination standard.

The accountancy body recommends that the average student needs 18 hours study (including class hours) per week over the academic year to pass each stage of the exams. In the meantime Brian approached the training officer within his organisation and was delighted to find out that the company was prepared to fund his studying provided he successfully passed each exam. In addition the company would grant him one week's study leave for each exam in addition to the examination leave necessary to actually sit the exams. The company would also be prepared to give Brian the necessary on-the-job financial experience to meet the practical entry criteria and work experience of the accountancy body.

Five years on Brian is a qualified accountant and is now a financial controller within his company. By focusing on written objectives and doing the necessary work to achieve them Brian has realised his ambition. His salary has increased substantially and his work is very satisfying and challenging. The commitment and hard study has paid off.

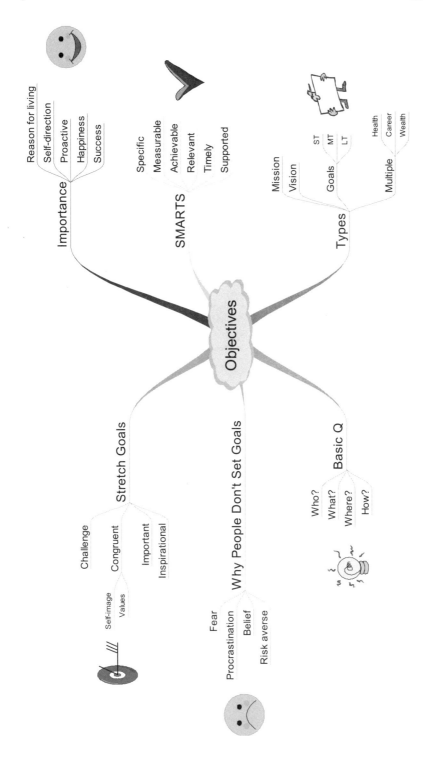

Objectives

Importance
- Reason for living
- Self-direction
- Proactive
- Happiness
- Success

SMARTS
- Specific
- Measurable
- Achievable
- Relevant
- Timely
- Supported

Types
- Mission
- Vision
- Goals
  - ST
  - MT
  - LT
- Multiple
  - Health
  - Career
  - Wealth

Stretch Goals
- Challenge
- Congruent
  - Self-image
  - Values
- Important
- Inspirational

Why People Don't Set Goals
- Fear
- Procrastination
- Belief
- Risk averse

Basic Q
- Who?
- What?
- Where?
- How?

2

PLANS

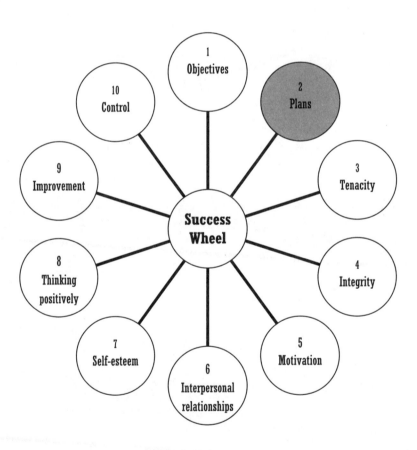

- ◆ What are the different types of plans?
- ◆ Why is planning important?
- ◆ What is the planning process?
- ◆ What are the barriers to planning?
- ◆ How can I apply planning to my life and work?

"An intelligent plan is the first step to success. The man who plans knows where he is going, knows what progress he is making and has a pretty good idea when he will arrive. Planning is the open road to your destination. If you don't know where you are going, how can you expect to get there?" — Basil S. Walsh

---

P stands for Plans and is the second letter of our acronym OPTIMISTIC. Without plans and action programmes our objectives will never be achieved. Planning ensures that you put your thoughts on paper and that everything is considered and nothing overlooked. There is a well-known systematic planning process that should be followed in all cases. The barriers to planning include lack of commitment and lack of confidence. Having a positive attitude to your work will make work more interesting and satisfying.

Importance of Planning

Planning is important for many reasons including the following:

- Planning puts your thoughts on paper. It ensures that the implications of everything are considered in detail and that nothing is overlooked. Action planning details the actions that must be performed to reach your goals. We need a blueprint to build a house. However few people realise that you need a plan to build a successful life.

- Planning provides a route map. A technique that is often used is called critical path analysis. This sets down the activities, events and time scale including start and completion times necessary for implementing your route map. It shows the critical items that must be done to achieve your objectives on target.

- Planning offers a control mechanism for comparing actual progress against targets for planning stages so that corrective action can be taken to put the plan back on target again while the implementation progresses. This feedback ensures that you are learning from your mistakes. Planning and control are known as the Siamese twins of management.

- Planning avoids hasty ill-considered decisions being taken. Alternative courses of action will be evaluated taking into account risk/return and the best choice in regard to feasibility and cost considerations. Without formal planning it is unlikely that alternative courses of action would be considered.

- Planning expands options and increases the ability to respond to change. Planning reduces uncertainty by generating information needed to successfully deal with anticipated problems and contingencies.

What Does Planning Involve?

Planning involves:

- Setting objectives and deciding what to do in the future by setting down the detailed steps needed.

- Deciding how to do it including methods, procedures, sequence and resources.

- Deciding the expertise you need to acquire to achieve your goals.

- Deciding when to do it including starting time, progress monitoring and completion times.

"Good plans shape good decisions. That's why good planning helps to make elusive dreams come true." — Lester R. Bittel

---

- Deciding who to do it with including identifying the people who are needed to help you with your plans. These might include colleagues, coaches and mentors.

- Determining the cost of achieving your objectives.

The ASPIRE Model

The ASPIRE model is an acronymic guide to self-development. Following the model should help you draw up plans to achieve your goals in life. ASPIRE stands for:

- **A**ssess your present position — clarify your vision, mission, values and goals. This has been dealt with in Chapter 1.

- **S**WOT — do a strengths, weaknesses, opportunities and threats analysis on yourself. Capitalise on your strengths and de-emphasise your weaknesses. Strengths might include your positive can-do attitude, special abilities, good experience, qualifications and high intelligence. Weaknesses might include a lack of certain skills, your tendency to harbour negative thoughts, be reactive, a perfectionist and to procrastinate. Take short courses to address any weaknesses such as time management, presentation, negotiation and assertiveness skills and to develop project management expertise. Assess your competencies, personality traits, abilities, interests and learning styles. Exploit opportunities and anticipate threats to the successful completion of your plans that may arise. See threats as possible challenges to be exploited. See problems as opportunities to learn. Frequently, opportunities come our way disguised as problems.

- **P**lan — draw up an action plan to achieve your short-term and long-term goals. Failure to plan is planning to fail. Set performance standards for each stage of the plan. These should have regard to quantity, quality, time-scale and cost. Plan the deployment of resources such as people and equipment needed for effective planning. Identify the tasks that must be completed to achieve each sub-goal. Estimate the approximate time to complete each task. Determine the order in which tasks will be completed. Have a target date for the completion of each task. Determine the critical path, which is the sequence of activities that take the longest time to complete. Any delay of activities on the critical path will delay the overall completion time of the project. Other activities are non-critical and can be delayed without delaying the overall project. Design contingency plans. Anything that can go wrong will go wrong and will probably do so at the worst possible time. Therefore plans should be adaptable and flexible enough to cater for unique circumstances and unforeseen difficulties.

- **I**mplement your plan — plan the work and work the plan. Take action. If you don't take action nothing is going to change or get done. The complexity of goals and how they are interrelated determines the order in which activities will be done. You might be able to accomplish some goals simultaneously and others sequentially.

- **R**eview — compare your progress against your performance standards and sub-goals. New obstacles may be identified and as a consequence new tactics needed. Circumstances may change demanding a revised approach. You will find out what works and what does not work as plans progress. Mid-course adjustments may be necessary to put things right. So take corrective action as appropriate to put your actual plans back on target again. Review is an ongoing process of continuous improvement against sub-goals until your desired end-goal is achieved. In general you should review your short-term goals every week, your medium-term goals every month, and your long-term goals every six months.

- **E**valuate — work out how successful you have been in achieving your personal development vision, mission and goals and take corrective action as appropriate. What can you learn from setbacks and mistakes? Scientists know that mistakes are just opportunities for learning — a part of the scientific experimentation process.

"Planning is bringing the future into the present so that you can do something about it now." — Alan Lakein

---

Barriers to Planning

The barriers to planning include the following:

- Lack of commitment and confidence, including fear of blame, and criticism in the event of you failing to effectively carry out your plans. The less confident you are the less likely you are to stick to your plan.

- Constraints such as lack of information and resources may stymie your plans. In practice plans usually take longer and cost more than you anticipated.

- Insufficient thought is put into the planning process so that time-scales and goals prove to be unrealistic.

- Lack of belief in plans. Many people hate planning because they think that the future is too uncertain and is therefore impossible to predict with any reasonable accuracy. They may consider planning to be a straitjacket that limits initiative and flexibility.

- An attitude that planning takes up too much time and interferes with the accomplishment of day-to-day responsibilities. In fact planning only takes up about 5 per cent of overall time and more than pays for itself in the resulting efficiency and effectiveness in the completion of tasks. Effectiveness is doing the right things and efficiency is doing them right.

- Lack of expertise. Some people don't know how to plan and are unaware of the systematic approach to planning and techniques such as the critical path method. Taking a training course in planning would address this problem.

A Planned Approach to Work

Much of the daily work we do is of a routine nature. No matter how high you progress in your organisation there will be routine aspects to your job. Keep the end result in sight all the time so that you understand that the routine is necessary to achieve desired outcomes. Think before you act and realise that success in doing anything is often in getting the detail right first.

You need to change your attitude towards your work and emphasise the challenging aspects rather than concentrating on the negative. This will improve your morale and make your work more satisfying. Continually see how the existing method of doing the work could be improved. Believe in the notion that there is a better way of doing everything. The concept of continuous improvement should be your goal. Set yourself the objective of being the best performer in this particular position to date. Looking for ways to improve the job will keep your powers of creativity alive and make the job more interesting.

> "We must discard the idea that past routine, past ways of doing things, are probably the best ways. On the contrary, we must assume there is probably a better way to do almost anything. We must stop assuming that a thing which has never been done before probably cannot be done at all." — Donald M. Nelson

Set up a dynamic daily routine so that you practise efficient habits and increase your productivity. Good habits eventually become automatic responses and will save you time. Negative habits have the opposite effect. Schedule time for rest, relaxation and exercise. Take periodic breaks to maximise your learning and productivity. Build up your self-esteem by writing down your accomplishments. Demonstrate how you are succeeding by charting your progress. Cherish positive feedback and use it to motivate yourself to higher standards of performance. Praise yourself as you complete your daily tasks. Positive self-affirmations will help your self-esteem.

"Our plans miscarry because they have no aim. When a man does not know what harbour he is making for, no wind is the right wind." —Seneca

---

Personal Development Plans (PDPs)

A personal development plan identifies your personal strengths and weaknesses, notes your training and development needs, and specifies goals for your self-development. The plan will help you clarify your hopes, ambitions, aspirations and expectations. It will promote self-responsibility and a sense of ownership for personal, educational, training and career development. If the company you work in hasn't a formal process in place you should draw up your own plan. After all, you are responsible for managing your own career. Don't let your career and chance or the whims of others govern development. Take control of your destiny and draw up your own personal development plan.

In order to do this you need certain information such as:

- What knowledge, skills and experience do I have now?

- What roles and jobs do they currently cater for?

- What is the next logical career progression for me?

- What competencies will I need to develop for this role?

- What training and experience do I need to acquire to develop these competencies?

- How long will it take to acquire the necessary training and experience?

Drawing Up a PDP

To draw up a personal development plan you need to:

1. Assess current position and future development needs. Compare the actual level of skills you have with the desired level of competencies that you need to progress to the next level.

2. Set learning goals. These might include improving performance in your existing job, improving or acquiring new skills and updating or acquiring new knowledge. New competencies may be needed to cope with change, new technology, new policies, procedures or products, or with a new job or promotional position.

3. Action plan. This is a detailed schedule setting out the activities needed to achieve your goals and specifying when and where they will take place. Nothing gets done until you actually do something. It is important that you identify the sources of support you'll need, such as coaching or mentoring, to help you on your way.

4. Implement your plan. Monitor progress on the journey to the achievement of your objectives. Compare actual results against targets at appropriate intervals and take corrective action as necessary to put the actual situation back on course.

5. Keep a learning log. This is a diary that you complete each week recording what you learned during the week. It will help you reflect on your experiences, learn from your mistakes, and develop new strategies for your development in the future. This reflection will increase your self-understanding and give you a sense of who you are, where you are currently and where you want to go in the future.

Summary

Planning puts your thoughts on paper and provides a route map towards your goals. Planning involves setting objectives and deciding what you need to do in the future to achieve them. The ASPIRE model is a systematic approach to personal planning. assess, SWOT analysis, plan, implement, review and evaluate.

Barriers to planning include lack of commitment and confidence. A positive attitude towards work will improve your morale and job satisfaction and keep you interested in your work. Personal development plans will help you plan your career in a thoughtful and systematic way.

FIVE STEPS TO MAKING BETTER PLANS

1. **Consider why planning is essential if you want goals to come to fruition. Write down two reasons why you should plan.**

2. **Write down what the acronym ASPIRE stands for. Consider each step and how you can use it to achieve your goals.**

3. **Write down two relevant barriers to planning and how you would overcome them.**

4. **Draw up a schedule of the actions you need to take to achieve your goals.**

5. **Using the guidelines in the chapter on personal development plans draw up your own PDP for your career and review it quarterly.**

Case Study: Planning

Helen emerged from her annual performance review feeling confident. She is an ambitious 30-year-old senior computer programmer, and had just finished her personal development plans with Ann, her supervisor. Her annual review was very positive in line with Helen's attitude and very good on-the-job performance. She displays initiative and gets projects done efficiently, on time and within budget. She gets along very well with her supervisor and other employees and is a good team player.

Helen prepared in advance what she was going to say at the appraisal meeting and concentrated on highlighting the positive aspects of her job performance during the year. In addition she had updated her personal development plans linking them to her career goals. Helen's goals were crystal clear and she set out in detail the planning process showing exactly how she intended to achieve them with the timescales involved.

- *Systems analyst within a year.*

- *Systems project team leader within two years.*

- *Manager of the information systems department within five years.*

Ann was impressed with Helen's clear thinking, as well as her concrete plans and commitment to achieving her goals. Ann admired her decisiveness in knowing exactly what she wanted to do, backed up by the appropriate plans to achieve her goals. These included enrolling in the coming year at the local college to do a BSc in computer science. This is a five-year part-time course run in the evenings from Monday to Friday and would require weekend study time as well. This demonstrates Helen's commitment to furthering her career. Helen is already a member of the Computer Society, a professional body for those involved in the computer industry. This helps her keep up to date with current and future developments in the profession through its monthly meetings with other computer professionals.

As part of her personal development plan Helen proposed in conjunction and in agreement with Ann to attend upcoming seminars and workshops run by the Computer Society and other computer training organisations during normal working hours. These courses link in to Helen's career plan and the work needs of the company. Helen was motivated by the words of the company's Human Resource Manager who said, "If you don't know where you want to go, you'll never get there." Helen has no intention of floating aimlessly through her career. She believes in shaping her own destiny through action plans and programmes. She doesn't wait around hoping that other people will look after her interests (they usually don't) but takes the initiative herself. She takes responsibility for her own career decisions. She knows that if its going to be it's up to her.

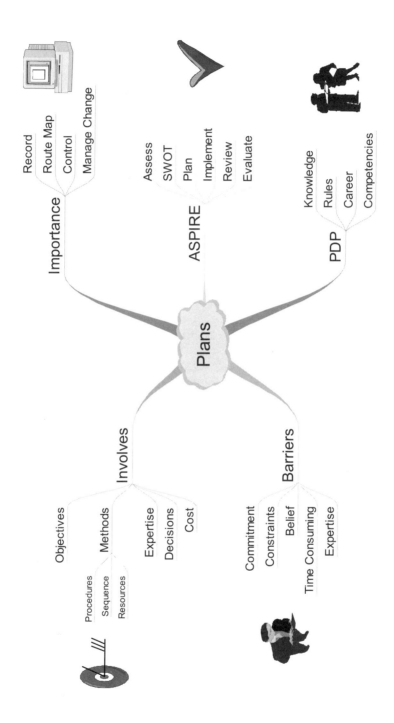

Plans

Importance
- Record
- Route Map
- Control
- Manage Change

ASPIRE
- Assess
- SWOT
- Plan
- Implement
- Review
- Evaluate

PDP
- Knowledge
- Rules
- Career
- Competencies

Involves
- Objectives
- Methods
  - Procedures
  - Sequence
  - Resources
- Expertise
- Decisions
- Cost

Barriers
- Commitment
- Constraints
- Belief
- Time Consuming
- Expertise

3

TENACITY

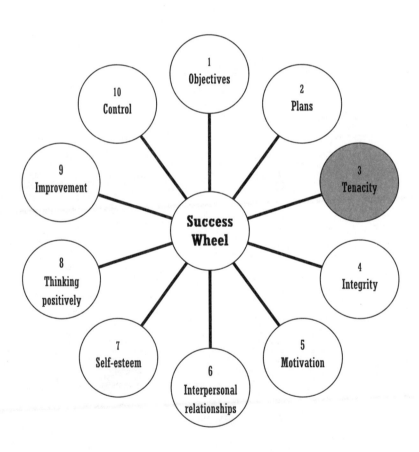

- ◆ Why is commitment important to success?
- ◆ Who are the exemplars of commitment?
- ◆ Why is patience important?
- ◆ Why do persistent people achieve their goals?
- ◆ What is resilience?

"Nothing in the world can take the place of persistence. Talent will not; nothing is more common than unsuccessful men with talent. Genius will not; unrewarded genius is almost a proverb. Education will not; the world is full of educated derelicts. Persistence and determination alone are omnipotent. The slogan 'Press on' has solved and always will solve the problems of the human race."
— Calvin Coolidge

T stands for tenacity and is the third letter of our acronym OPTIMISTIC. Tenacity is the capacity to be very determined and to stick firmly to a decision, plan or opinion. Commitment, persistence, patience, resilience and stamina should underpin and reinforce tenacity. Commitment has been defined as being devoted or dedicated to a cause, person or relationship. Persistence is the quality of continuing steadily despite problems or obstacles. Patience is the capacity to endure waiting or delay without becoming annoyed or upset or to persevere calmly when faced with difficulties. Resilience is the ability to recover quickly and bounce back from setbacks without getting stressed. Stamina is the enduring physical or mental energy and strength that allows a person to do something for a long time.

Commitment

Being committed means that you are pledged, obligated or emotionally driven towards your purpose or goal. Committed people are prepared to do what is needed and make personal sacrifices to get the job done. They refuse to make excuses and quit when problems arise but instead focus on finding solutions. Commitment is demonstrated by action. Words are cheap. When you are truly committed you begin to see and attract the resources around you to achieve your goals.

People who succeed in life and realise their goals make the appropriate decisions to do so and then stick to them. On his first attempt Sir Edmund Hillary failed to conquer Mount Everest. After this attempt he is reputed to have said, "Mount Everest, you have defeated me once and you might defeat me again. But I'm coming back again and again, and I'm going to win because you've grown all that you are going to grow and I'm still growing." Hillary realised that he was getting better all the time and learning from his mistakes. He knew that he would eventually succeed. True to his word, Sir Edmund Hillary was the first to reach the summit of Mount Everest, the highest point on Earth, on 29 May 1953.

Mahatma Gandhi, though one of the gentlest of men, used great determination and commitment to win independence for India from Britain without striking a single blow. He used non-violent methods such as non-cooperation, including hunger strikes and passive resistance, to achieve his aims. He was a man of very strong convictions who believed that social and political progress could be achieved through peaceful means. Gandhi's life is a testament to the fact that one totally committed person can change the course of a nation's history. He brought the mighty British Empire to its knees.

Persistence

Persistent people keep going when everything seems lost. When the going gets tough, persistent people get going. They refuse to take no for an answer and if at first they don't succeed they try another approach. They take rejections in their stride. They accept that there are going to be ups and downs in life and that you must be able to take the rough with the smooth. They are propelled forward by a positive self-image and a strong self-belief. They know what they have to do and know that they are capable of doing it.

"Let me tell you the secret that has led me to my goal. My strength lies solely in my tenacity." — Louis Pasteur

---

Many people born with enormous advantages throw them away, while others who start out confronted with seemingly insurmountable obstacles often succeed beyond expectation. Noël Coward said, "Thousands of people have talent. I might as well congratulate you for having eyes in your head. The one and only thing that counts is, do you have staying power?" Willpower is where you refuse to accept the limitations of a situation and resolve to do something about it. Just like muscles, the more you use your willpower the stronger it gets.

There is no such thing as an overnight success. People who succeed have years of dedicated experience and practice behind them. People see the extraordinary feats and talents of others but not the hidden countless hours of hard work that went into producing them. They overestimate the role of talent while underestimating the role of dedicated work in creating them. When you watch a concert pianist you are probably viewing two decades of conscientious practice. The only place success comes before work is in the dictionary. Nothing in the world can take the place of order, discipline, common sense, consistency, passion, persistence and hard work.

A good athlete knows it takes persistence and a "second wind" to overcome physical fatigue before they can bounce back. The horse with stamina and the rider with persistence of purpose often excel. The average student with persistence often succeeds where the brilliant student without the same resolve fails. People who persisted in their efforts and became successful are drawn from all walks of life including inventors, writers, politicians, employees, the elderly and even the unemployed.

Famous Persistent People

- Thomas Alva Edison (1847-1931) was one of the most prolific and persistent inventors of all time. He invented the phonograph in 1877 and the electric light bulb in 1878. He also introduced one of the first cinema projectors and improved Alexander Bell's telephone. Edison tried 10,000 times before he produced the first electric light bulb. He did not view such attempts as failures but as experiments and learning opportunities helping him along the way in reaching his goal of producing an electric light bulb. During his career he used his indomitable spirit, passion, persistence, can-do attitude and optimism to produce more than 1,000 patents. He said that many of life's failures are people who did not realise how close they were to success when they gave up.

"Results! Why, man, I have got a lot of results. I know several thousand things that won't work." — Thomas Edison

---

- Nelson Mandela became the first black president of South Africa in 1994. He was an active member of the African National Congress who opposed apartheid. In 1964 he was sentenced to life imprisonment for treason. From within the prison system he continued his campaign against apartheid and never gave up hope of being successful. After a long international campaign he was released in 1990, having become a symbol of resistance to apartheid throughout the world. In 1993 he was awarded the Nobel Peace Prize jointly with de Klerk. Mandela has shown character, determination and persistence in his long fight for freedom for the black people in South Africa. Mandela showed tremendous will-power and courage in the face of adversity.

"Most of the important things in the world have been accomplished by people who have kept on trying when there seemed to be no hope at all" — Dale Carnegie

---

- Abraham Lincoln became President of the United States in 1860 on an anti-slavery ticket after a persistent struggle to get there. He had suffered years of personal setbacks, sickness, trauma and defeats on his journey to the presidency. His term of office was consumed by the civil war against the Southern states who were in favour of slavery and who had withdrawn from the Union following his election. He once said, "I am a slow walker, but I never walk backwards."

- In 1962, a nuclear war seemed imminent. The USA and the Soviet Union were in confrontation over the Cuban missile crisis. The US considered ways to communicate in the event of a nuclear attack. Paul Baran, a researcher at RAND Corporation, offered a solution. He suggested a more robust communications network using "redundancy" and "digital" technology. He had conceived the Internet's architecture at the height of the cold war. Baran's ideas were dismissed as impracticable. He countered by writing a series of technical papers to answer criticisms of his ideas and further develop his thoughts. Baran and his colleagues at RAND persisted and their efforts eventually became the foundation for the World Wide Web. Baran later recalled, "Many of the things I thought possible would tend to sound like utter nonsense, or impractical depending on the generosity of spirit in those brought up in an earlier world."

- Tawni O'Dell received 300 rejection slips before she finally became a published author. Her 2001 debut novel *Back Roads* got great reviews in the press and also won a coveted spot in Oprah Winfrey's world-renowned book club. It rose to number two on the New York Times Best Seller List, where it remained for eight weeks. In an interview Tawni gave the fol-

lowing advice: "Never give up on your dream. Talent is a ne-
cessity but only part of what goes into making a successful
writer. Perseverance is all-important. If you don't have the
desire and the belief in yourself to keep trying after you have
been told you should quit, you'll never make it."

- A fusion of passion, single-mindedness and perseverance
  will see you through in the end. In 1994 Princeton Professor
  Andrew Wiles completed one of the most extraordinary
  journeys in the history of mathematics. For more than thirty
  years, Wiles had been obsessed with Fermat's Last Theorem,
  a seemingly simple problem that had beaten mathematicians
  for 350 years. Wiles encountered the problem when he was
  only 10 years old. He knew all the great mathematicians in
  history couldn't solve it and he resolved that he would be the
  one to do so. In 1993, after seven years of intense work —
  more than 15,000 hours — Wiles presented his completed
  proof of Fermat's Last Theorem at a conference in England.
  However, a handful of peer reviewers found several small er-
  rors. Wiles didn't lose heart but took another year to address
  them. The Princeton professor attributes his achievement to
  his persistence rather than to his brains.

Patience

Patience is the capacity to endure delay without becoming annoyed, upset or angry and to persevere calmly when faced with
difficulties or provocation. The fable about the golden goose
illustrates the point. The farmer had a goose that laid a golden
egg each day. However the farmer was selfish, impatient and
wanted to get rich quick. So he decided to kill the goose and
get all the eggs at once. He opened the goose to find nothing.
The result was no more goose and no more golden eggs.

Habits of patience, acceptance and forbearance will make
your passage through life easier. A broken leg takes on average eight to ten weeks to heal. Nature just takes its course and
there is nothing you can do about it but just be patient. Patience
is enjoying the moment and the journey of getting there. Most
of us reach our goals eventually if we take the appropriate ac-

tion. All things are difficult before they become easy. John Ruskin said "On the whole, it is patience which makes the final difference between those who succeed or fail in all things. All the greatest people have it in an infinite degree, and among the less, the patient weak ones always conquer the impatient strong". If success were easy everybody would be successful. Nothing can take the place of patience.

"Patience and tenacity of purpose are worth more than twice their weight of cleverness." — Thomas Henry Huxley

---

Patience brings its rewards eventually. Those who invest in a diversified portfolio of shares on the stock market for the long term usually reap the rewards. They know that there is no such thing as getting rich overnight but are prepared to wait for the long-term benefits. They know good companies with good products and good management will make money and in the long run their shares will appreciate. In the meantime there will be highs and lows but over the long term patience will pay off.

Most Quitters Fail

Most people don't give themselves a chance and quit before they should. John Creasey, a popular British mystery writer, got 743 rejections before he published his first book. He subsequently went on to have a long and very successful career as a writer. He certainly showed unusual persistence in his goal to be a published writer. Every year thousands of new businesses are set up. The vast majority will fail. Five years on only a small number will still be in business. The major problem is that those who meet obstacles haven't the determination and self-belief to persist with their goals. They often give up on the brink of success.

Most people who start a distance learning programme or night classes quit. As a former college lecturer I found that there was standing room only at the start of courses. At the end of the academic year you'd find that about 60 per cent or more who had taken up the programme had left. Similarly, many people who start university quit. It doesn't mean all of these are failures. There are exceptions like Bill Gates, the founder of Microsoft, who quit college but went on to become a renowned success. In fact there are times when quitting is the right thing to do. If you are in a house that is on fire the smart thing to do is to get out as quickly as possible. Many of those who perished in Hurricane Katrina in New Orleans in September 2005 refused to leave their homes despite adequate warnings of the imminent disaster and paid the price with their lives.

**"Few things are impossible to diligence and skill; great works are performed not by strength, but by perseverance."
— Samuel Johnson**

Most people who start out in a selling career quit. They find it difficult to handle constant rejection and just give up. Those who persist go on to develop very successful selling careers. The average person who sets out to play a musical instrument quits. In the accountancy profession most students who set out on the road with initial enthusiasm quit after setbacks such as failing a particular stage of the examinations. Successful people know that the secret of success is persistence. Instead of seeing setbacks as overwhelming, they see them as temporary events that can be overcome.

Resolutions

Psychologists have found that 40 per cent of people who make New Year resolutions are still going strong six months into the new-year. However, around 50 per cent have already given up by the end of January. It seems getting past the first month with your resolution intact predicts long-term success. Quitters only hurt themselves. They are quickly forgotten about. Only the successful are remembered. Anyone contemplating quitting should consider the following poem written by some unknown author:

The world won't cry if you quit
And the world won't whine if you fail;
The busy world won't notice it,
No matter how loudly you wail.

Nobody will worry that you
Have relinquished the fight and gone down
For it's only the things that you do
That are worthwhile and get you renown.

The quitters are quickly forgotten
On them the world spends little time
And a few never care that you hadn't
The courage or patience to climb.

So give up and quit in despair
And take your place back on the shelf;
But don't think the world is going to care;
You are injuring only yourself.

Resilience

Resilience is the ability to bounce back, survive and flourish from the trials, tribulations and challenges of life. It is the strength to start all over again and overcome grief, pain, sickness, trauma, obstacles and frustrations. Resilient people are able to take hardship, adversity, disappointment, misfortune, bereavement, and criticism in their stride. They willingly engage with and overcome life's challenges. They tend to be more energetic, purposeful and persistent in the pursuit of their goals. They trust themselves to make the right decisions even when advised otherwise. It is known that resilience is related to confidence, self-efficacy, flexibility and optimism.

Resilient people accept that frustration is part of the human condition. Nobody is exempt from disappointment, pain and suffering in this world. When confronted with difficulties they have the attitude that things could have gone better but they could be worse. They try to see the bright side and can often see the humour in the absurdities and contradictions of life. They are grateful for what they have. They consider where they started from and appreciate how much they have accomplished in life so far. They do not spend time making unfavourable comparisons with others but instead get on with what they have to do. They realise that out of adversity sometimes comes strength and greatness.

**"Patience and perseverance have a magical effect before which difficulties disappear and obstacles vanish."
— John Quincy Adams**

Resilient people realise that they can't do it alone and need the love and support of other people to get back on track again. They are able to keep things in perspective and maintain a hopeful outlook. The more positive one's attitude the more one can withstand both the expected and unexpected slings and arrows of life. Resilient people externalise blame and internalise success. Successful people have the resilience to take risk and accept some failure.

Transform Negative Experiences into Positive Ones

Resilient people learn from negative experiences and transform them into positive ones. They are less likely to suffer from anxiety and depression. They reframe anxiety in a positive light as excitement. They are thus able to muster the strength to change direction in life when things go wrong and a chosen path becomes blocked or non-productive. The Alcoholics Anonymous serenity prayer is very appropriate in this context and goes as follows: "Grant me the serenity to accept the things I cannot change, the courage to change the things I can and the wisdom to know the difference."

Many people have the resilience to turn setbacks and handicaps into victories and opportunities for growth. Consider all the business people who have suffered bankruptcy only to come through more determined and ultimately more successful. Many people from dysfunctional families grow up with a healthy disposition and live happy and productive lives. Bates (2005) reports that one study of children in Kauai identified a group of such high-risk children and followed their life course for 30 years to adulthood. Despite having parents with mental illness, being socially and economically disadvantaged, one-third of these children grew up to be confident, competent parents.

"You've done it before and you can do it now. See the positive possibilities. Redirect the substantial energy of your frustration and turn it into positive, effective, unstoppable determination." — Ralph Marston

---

Building the Strengths of Resilience

Blum (1998) reports on the key aspects of resilience research:

- There is no timeline and set period for finding strength, resilient behaviours and coping skills. People do best if they develop strong coping skills as children, and some researchers suggest the first ten years are the best time to do so. But the ability to turn around is always there at any stage of our lives.

- Faith — be it in the future or in the world or in a higher power — is an essential ingredient. Ability to perceive bad times as temporary rather than permanent is an essential strength.

- Most resilient people rely on support systems. One of the important findings of resilience research is that people who cope well with adversity, even if they don't have a strong family support system, are able to ask for help or recruit others to help them. This is true for children and adults; resilient adults, for instance, are far more likely to talk to friends and even co-workers about difficult events in their lives.

- Setting goals and planning for the future is a strong factor in dealing with adversity. In fact, as University of California psychologist Emmy Werner points out, it may minimise the adversity itself. For instance, Werner found that when Hurri-

cane Iniki battered Hawaii in 1993, islanders who were previously identified as resilient reported less property damage than others in the study. The reason for this is that they
had planned and prepared more, boarded up windows, and
had adequate insurance. Being prepared for disaster les-
sons the impact when it finally occurs.

- Believing in oneself and recognising one's strengths is important. University of Alabama psychologist Ernestine
  Brown discovered that when children of depressed, barely
  functioning mothers, took pride in helping take care of the
  family, they didn't feel as trapped. Brown says, "You pick
  yourself up, give yourself value. If you can't change a bad
  situation, you can at least nurture yourself. Make yourself a
  place for intelligence and competence, surround yourself
  with things that help you stabilise, and remember what
  you're trying to do".

- And it's equally important to actually recognise one's own
  strengths. Many people don't. Self-recognition can be taught
  and will help adults build a newly resilient approach to life.

Resilient People

Brody (2005) reports that until recently resilience was thought
to be an entirely inborn trait but it is now realised that it can be
nurtured and learnt. Resilient children are not invulnerable to
trauma or immune to suffering. But they bounce back. They find
ways to cope, set goals and achieve them despite myriad obstacles like drug-addicted parents, dire poverty or physical
disabilities thrown in their path. Dr Robert Brooks of Harvard
and Dr Sam Goldstein of the University of Utah maintain that being resilient does not mean a life without risks or adverse conditions but rather learning how to deal effectively with the inevitable strains and stresses of life.

People who lack resilience are less able to rise above adversity or learn from their mistakes and move on. Instead of focusing on what they can control and accepting responsibility for
their lives, they waste time and energy on matters beyond their
influence. As a result, the circumstances of their lives leave them

feeling helpless and hopeless and prone to depression. When things go wrong or don't work out as expected, they tend to think, "I can't do this" or even worse, "It can't be done".

Brody (2005) also reports that Dr Wendy Schlessel Harpham, a Dallas physician, wife and mother of three, is the epitome of resilience. Struck with a recurring cancer in her thirties that required a decade of debilitating treatments, she was forced to give up medical practice. She turned instead to writing books and lecturing to professional and lay audiences to help millions of others and their families through the cancer experience.

"Tenacity is a pretty fair substitute for bravery, and the best form of tenacity I know is expressed in a Danish fur trapper's principle: 'The next mile is the only one a person really has to make'." — Eric Sevareid

---

By the time Orison Swett Marden was 32 he was the owner of a chain of hotels. He was determined to help others and for the next decade he collected notes of inspirational stories to help people make their way successfully in the world. In 1890 disaster struck when his manuscript was destroyed in a fire. Instead of bemoaning the loss, he decided to reconstruct his work. His book called *Pushing to the Front*, a collection of the life stories of great men, went on to become a bestseller. The success of the book prompted him to start a magazine called *Success.* On the cover of the earliest magazines, Marden defined success as "Education, enterprise, enthusiasm, energy, economy, self-respect, self-reliance, self-help and self-culture". It was a journal of inspiration, encouragement, progress and self-help.

Leavy (2002) tells the story of a Texan named George Dawson who died in 2001 at the age of 103. This is remarkable enough, but what is more remarkable was the fact that George started to learn how to read when he was 93. It shows that it is never too late to learn. Not only that but he went on to write a book, called *Life Is So Good*, sharing tidbits of wisdom while outlining his incredible journey through life. This journey kept him out of school as a boy because he had to work to support the family. We can all learn from the example of Dawson, who was a glowing testament to the power of perseverance and re-silience. He didn't just learn to read, but has become a model of inspiration for all those who can't read and are afraid to take the first step and simply try.

Stamina

Success has a price tag. That price tag is risk, endurance, pain, hard work, possible failure and many disappointments on the way. Successful people put in long hours to achieve their ambitions. The overnight success is a myth. To quote from Long-fellow's "Ladder of Saint Augustine":

> The heights by great men reached and kept
> Were not attained by sudden flight
> But they, while their companions slept,
> Were toiling upward in the night.

Nobody has shown more stamina and endurance that Lance Armstrong, the US cyclist who has won the Tour de France seven times from 1999 to 2005. This is an amazing feat in itself but is more astounding when you consider that Armstrong got testicular cancer that almost killed him. He had a cancerous tes-ticle removed but doctors found that the cancer had spread to his lungs, abdomen and brain. Armstrong had to endure much pain and a most aggressive form of chemotherapy to cure the disease. Nevertheless, he came back to competitive sport stronger and more determined than before. The old saying that out of adversity comes strength surely applies to Armstrong. During this time he set up the Lance Armstrong Foundation, which has raised million of dollars for cancer victims.

Armstrong now maintains that the cancer was the best thing that ever happened to him. He felt that enduring the pain of the Tour de France would be nothing in comparison to the pain he endured with the chemotherapy. Before becoming ill, he didn't care about strategy, tactics or teamwork — the things you need to master before you become a great cyclist. Before he had cancer he was a difficult person to deal with and argued all the time. He never trained right and just relied on his natural gift. During his convalescence he resolved to change his ways.

Terry Fox (1958-1981) was very athletic from a young age. Sadly, in 1977 Terry was diagnosed with a rare form of bone cancer. As a result his right leg had to be amputated six inches above the knee. Terry was no quitter and during his recovery developed the idea of a marathon run across Canada to raise money for cancer research. The run was called the Marathon of Hope. He began the run on the 12 April 1980. On 1 September, after 143 days of relentless pace and 5,373 kilometres, cancer was discovered in his lungs and he was forced to abandon the run. However, in the meantime his great stamina, despite a disability, had won the admiration and inspired a nation and the world. Terry died on 28 June 1981, one month before his 23rd birthday. His dream to collect $1 from every Canadian was more than realised. To date $250 million has been raised for cancer research. To commemorate his great deed, a mountain in British Columbia was named after him and he was made a Companion of the Order of Canada. Hundreds of runs are now held in Canada and throughout the world each year to raise money for cancer research.

Summary

Being committed means you are pledged, obligated or emotionally driven towards your goal. People who succeed in life and realise their goals make the appropriate decisions and follow them through with dedication and persistence.

Persistent people keep going when all seems lost. They refuse to take no for an answer and if at first they don't succeed they try another approach. Patient people have the capacity and stoicism to endure delay and take things in their stride. They realise that patience is often the defining characteristic between those who succeed and those who fail. Most people don't give themselves the chance and quit before they should, often on the brink of success.

Resilience is the ability to bounce back from difficulties, survive and flourish. Resilient people learn from negative experiences and transform them into positive ones. Successful people have great reserves of stamina and never give up until their goals have been achieved.

FIVE STEPS TO IMPROVING YOUR TENACITY

1. **Reflect on what commitment means to you and write down two reasons why committed people usually succeed in achieving their goals.**

2. **Write down two reasons why some people quit rather than persist when pursuing their goals.**

3. **Write down two ways in which you can build the strengths of resilience.**

4. **Dale Carnegie said that "most of the important things in the world have been accomplished by people when there seemed to be no hope at all". Reflect on two examples of famous people who persisted against the odds in pursuing their goals. These can be used as inspirational role models.**

5. **Consider your own strengths and recognise how they can be developed with patience to achieve your goals. Write down two reasons why there is no such thing as an overnight success.**

Case Study: Learning to Bounce Back

Greg, an outstanding football player in his day, was appointed manager of a local football club. The team was at the bottom of the league table and had been for a number of years. Support for the team had fallen away as was evidenced by the reduced attendance at matches. The previous manager had a tough, no-nonsense approach to the management of the players and believed in criticism rather than praise. When the team lost a game he concentrated on their shortcomings. He often shouted abuse at the players and had no hesitation in criticising them and pointing out their faults and failures in front of other team members. He continually compared them unfavourably with better players and teams in the league. There is no doubt this had a demoralising effect on the players.

When Greg took over he noticed that any time the opposing side scored a goal the body language of his team became very downcast and negative, and predicted the inevitable outcome — that they were going to lose the game. In the dressing room after the game there was an atmosphere of doom and gloom and self-pity. This worked like a self-fulfilling prophecy for future games with the inevitable outcome of more lost games.

Greg set out to build up the confidence, self-image and self-esteem of the team and improve their morale. He told them that goals would be conceded from time to time but they should learn to look on the bright side of things. They should see such events not as failures but as opportunities to show strength and resilience in the face of adversity and learn from their mistakes. They must bounce back and learn to turn negative situations into positive ones. They must learn how to take the rough with the smooth and learn how to handle defeat as well as victory.

Although skill, practice and luck play a part, most games were in fact won and lost in the heads of players. A positive mental approach was half the battle. Greg started to use the video of previous games to analyse to the team where they went wrong and to learn from their mistakes. He tried to anticipate the style of the opposition by studying previous games they played with other teams. Videos were also used to point out what went right and to reinforce good playing tactics within the team. He praised team members for good performance and constructively criticised those who were playing badly. Critical feedback to players was always done in private. Greg's primary objective was to build up the confidence of the team and maximise their strengths and minimise their weaknesses by analysing what went wrong and taking corrective action so that performance would be improved in the future. He always stressed the positive aspects of their play.

Greg tirelessly worked on the players to build their resilience, self-belief and self-esteem. He improved the training facilities and equipment. He also introduced new methods of training and tactics and strategy into their playing. In the home ground, he improved the dressing room facilities and installed the best showering and bathing facilities. Within a few months morale of the team had improved beyond recognition and the team was winning and within a few months was near the top of the league table. Defeats were now rare and when they happened the team focused on their strengths and what they needed to do to improve their next game rather than concentrating continually on their shortcomings. The support for the team had increased considerably and this was reflected in the increased cash taken at the gate.

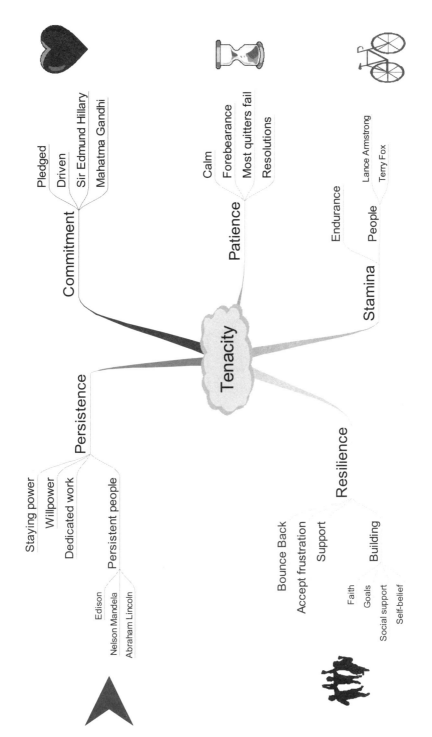

Tenacity

Commitment
- Pledged
- Driven
- Sir Edmund Hillary
- Mahatma Gandhi

Patience
- Calm
- Forebearance
- Most quitters fail
- Resolutions

Stamina
- Endurance
- People
  - Lance Armstrong
  - Terry Fox

Persistence
- Staying power
- Willpower
- Dedicated work
- Persistent people
  - Edison
  - Nelson Mandela
  - Abraham Lincoln

Resilience
- Bounce Back
- Accept frustration
- Support
- Building
  - Faith
  - Goals
  - Social support
  - Self-belief

4

INTEGRITY

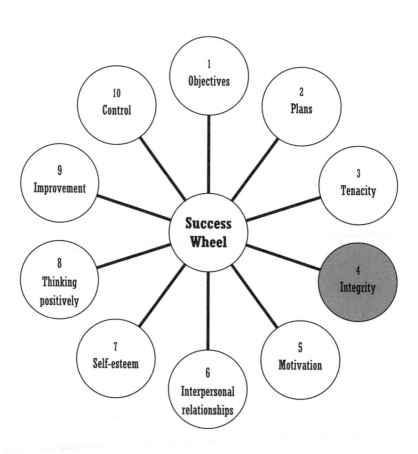

- ◆ What is a personal code of ethics?
- ◆ What do we mean by good character?
- ◆ What are the classic virtues?
- ◆ Why is trust so important?

"Good character is that quality which makes one dependable whether being watched or not, which makes one truthful when it is to one's advantage to be a little less than truthful, which makes one courageous when faced with great obstacles, which endows one with the firmness of wise self-discipline." — Arthur S. Adams

---

I is for integrity and is the fourth letter of our acronym OPTIMISTIC. Sticking to a personal code of good ethics will help you lead a successful and rewarding life. Character means that you are guided in life by values of integrity, sincerity and fairness. The classic virtues of character are fortitude, temperance, prudence and justice. Many of the great and famous have fallen to earth because of poor character. There can be no lasting relationships without trust.

Personal Code of Ethics

A personal code of ethics lays down the principles and values that will guide your conduct and behaviour throughout life. Ethics are moral principles, ideals, values or rules of conduct that guide people to deal fairly with others. Ethics deal with what is right or wrong or with moral duties and obligations. Personal ethics is about the universal principles of justice, honesty, sincerity, integrity, truth, fairness, compassion, and respect for people's feelings, privacy, dignity and property. At a personal level if something bothers your conscience and you feel guilty about doing it, then don't do it.

Values are precepts that we hold dear or believe to be intrinsically desirable. Values are acquired or learned. Our values are a reflection of who we are and how we behave at any moment in time. Values are the philosophy that drive and guide our life and determine what we want and don't want. Without values we have no principles or priorities for how to lead a good life, or how to build a personal vision and goals. A personal code of ethics will include things like:

- Taking responsibility for your own actions

- Following the precept that honesty is the best policy

- Believing that human life is precious

- Keeping your promises

- Practising what you preach

- Doing what is right rather than what is expedient

- Practising courtesy, consideration and respect in your dealings with others

- Having respect for the rights of others, for the dignity of others and for the feelings of others

- Having respect for people generally and especially for the old, sick and disabled

- Having respect for the property of others.

Character

Character is about practising integrity, truth, honesty, sincerity, thoughtfulness, humility, kindness, good manners and compassion. Persons of good character know the difference between right and wrong. Integrity is a journey, not a destination. You will need to update your personal ethics in line with changing circumstances. What is right today might be wrong tomorrow.

Honesty and integrity go together. There are no half measures. It cannot be turned off and on like a tap. Lack of integrity leads to fraud, corruption, bribery, dishonesty, forgery, greed, lies and deception. Dishonesty and the perpetual need to cover up deceit makes lives complicated and results in anxiety, stress, apprehension, poor relationships, isolation and guilt. This is the burden that one has to carry for the legacy of unethical behaviour.

> **"Our character . . . is an omen of our destiny, and the more integrity we have and keep, the simpler and nobler that destiny is likely to be." — George Santayana**

Many ethical lapses stem from an oversized ego. Arrogant executives think they are untouchable and exempt from the rules and standards that apply to the rest of us. This may result in their downfall. Humble people control their ego and take a realistic view of their problems. They learn how to listen and admit that they haven't all the answers. They are prepared to swallow their pride and learn from others. One of the best ways to learn is to reflect on your experience and the experiences of others. Sir Isaac Newton, one of the world's greatest scientists, said near the end of his life, "I feel like a little child playing by the seashore while the great ocean of truth lies undiscovered before me". Dr Albert Einstein was also known for his childlike simplicity.

A Sense of Values

Aristotle believed a person's past behaviours were a good predictor of future actions. A person who demonstrates poor character in the past is likely to act unethically in the future. On the other hand, a person who has demonstrated good character in the past is likely to act with integrity in the future. Originally, character was the distinctive stamp that ancient brick-makers placed on their bricks. The stamp was the personal signature of the individual guaranteeing the quality and integrity of the brick-maker's work. Today character represents our individual stamp on our actions and personality. The stamp of good character is evidenced by the practice of integrity.

People's goals should be congruent with their values. For peace of mind you should live by your values and never compromise. Decisions should be in harmony with your principles and values. You should have the courage to live by your values, take risks and make mistakes, ask for help when needed and accept change as required. The value choice of honesty and integrity faces us every day. Paying taxes, telling the truth, keeping our promises, treating people with dignity, giving back too much change and giving accurate information are just some of the situations we frequently encounter.

The ancient Greeks believed that the classic virtues of a good person were fortitude, temperance, prudence and justice. Fortitude is the courage to persevere in the face of adversity. Temperance is self-restraint in the face of temptation. These days it includes being able to handle alcohol in a responsible manner and to be sensible in our sexual conduct. Prudence is practical wisdom and the ability to make wise decisions. Justice is fairness, honesty, truthfulness and observing the law in society.

Importance of Character

Character is the foundation stone on which respect is built. Character is built and nurtured by our early experiences in school and in the home. The adversities and hard knocks of life may contribute to forming good character or indeed may reinforce a bad one in response to perceived injustices. If lost, a good name is very difficult to recover.

> **"Character cannot be developed in ease and quiet. Only through experience of trial and suffering can the soul be strengthened, vision cleared, ambition inspired, and success achieved." — Helen Keller**

When character is destroyed, one of your most precious possessions is gone. Study great people and literature to gain a true insight and understanding of character. Churchill succinctly defined the case for character as "Never give in, never give in, never, never, never, never — in nothing, great or small, large or petty — never give in except to convictions of honour and good sense". We can also learn from the behaviour of the good, the bad and the ugly as analysed in all good novels.

Character is more important than education. It is not inherited but must be developed. However, when cultivated you have it for life. Habits are the foundation to a good character. Habits are defined as behaviour patterns that become regular or spontaneous due to repetition. Habits increase in strength over time and become ingrained in our subconscious to appear on cue as a conditioned response. To cultivate a habit you must repeat it often enough until it is taken over by the subconscious mind. Habits are important in the formation of character as emphasised in the following poem, whose source is unknown.

> Sow a thought and you reap an act:
> Sow an act and you reap a habit;
> Sow a habit and you reap a character;
> Sow a character and you reap a destiny.

Opinions alter, but character remains intact. Nobody can exceed the limitations of their character. Character is the investment that is worth most. It cannot be bought or sold but must be earned. A person's true worth can be measured by their character and not by what they wear or the size of their bank account.

"The measure of a man's real character is what he would do if he knew he would never be found out." — Thomas B. Macaulay

---

The best thing you can leave to posterity when you die is your character and good example. Your character is demonstrated by the quality of your relationships with others, especially in how you deal with those who are less privileged than you.

The Character Creed

The following character creed is from an unknown author but is worth reflecting on:

I believe in the supreme worth of the individual and in his right to life, liberty, and the pursuit of happiness.

I believe that every right implies a responsibility; every opportunity, an obligation; every possession, a duty.

I believe that the law was made for man, not man for the law; that government is the servant of the people, not the master.

I believe in the dignity of labour, whether with head or hand; that the world owes no man a living, but that it owes every man an opportunity to make a living.

I believe that thrift is essential to well-ordered living and that economy is a prime requisite of a sound financial structure, whether in government, business or personal affairs.

I believe that truth and justice are fundamental to an enduring social order.

I believe in the sacredness of a promise, that a man's word should be as good as his bond; that character — not wealth or power or position — is of supreme worth.

I believe that the rendering of useful service is the common duty of mankind and that only in the purifying fire of sacrifice is the dross of selfishness consumed and the greatness of the human soul set free.

I believe in the all-wise and all-loving God, named by whatever name, and that the individual's highest fulfilment, greatest happiness, and widest usefulness are to be found in living in harmony with His will.

I believe that love is the greatest thing in the world; it alone can overcome hate; right can and will triumph over might.

Lies and Deceit

Lying has long become an accepted part of everyday life. Most people find it hard to get through a day without lying. Kornet (1997) reports that most people lie once or twice a day. Both men and women lie in approximately a fifth of their social exchanges lasting ten or more minutes. Over the course of a week they deceive about 30 per cent of those they have contact with. They lie when they turn up late for work. Lawyers construct far-fetched theories on behalf of their clients or reporters misrepresent themselves in order to gain access to good stories. Lies are more likely to be told over the phone, which provides more anonymity than a face-to-face conversation.

"Each time you are honest and conduct yourself with honesty, a success force will drive you toward greater success. Each time you lie, even with a little white lie, there are strong forces pushing you toward failure." — Joseph Sugarman

---

Even political leaders lie. In the Watergate affair burglaries were authorised and sanctioned by President Nixon. Months of congressional hearings, testimony and denials by the president and his staff concluded with Nixon's resignation to avoid impeachment and various jail sentences for many of his closest associates. He is reputed to have said, "I was not lying, I said things that later on seemed to be untrue". President Clinton was threatened with impeachment for his sexual adventures with Monica Lewinsky. Under oath, he engaged in half-truths, lies and deceptions to conceal the affair.

During election campaigns politicians make promises that they have no intention of keeping. They operate on the principle that promises are made to be broken. As soon as they are elected their commitments to their electorate are quickly forgotten. In fact the term "you sound like a politician" has gone into everyday vocabulary meaning to be deceitful and unreliable.

Business Lies

Being economical with the truth, though widespread in politics and business, is not synonymous with having a good character. Being Machiavellian or practising elaborate cunning rituals or deceitfulness to get ahead in life may reap short-term dividends but is unlikely to be a successful strategy in the long term. Lies often come back to haunt people. People of character match their words with their behaviour. Hypocrisy is not a defining characteristic of decent people.

"A single lie destroys a whole reputation of integrity."
— Baltasar Gracian

In the business world, many reputations have been destroyed and lives ruined because of lies, greed and corruption. It seems personal ethics goes out the window when it comes to business. One of the most notorious was the case of Ivan Boesky and his insider trading scams. At one stage in his career he made a speech at a business graduation ceremony in the University of California where he claimed that "Greed is all right . . . I think greed is healthy." Later on, he was arrested, tried, fined $100 million and convicted and spent some time in jail. So much for his concept of "Greed is good". This type of behaviour is always a personal tragedy and may be the end of a promising career.

Nick Leeson is infamous as the man who brought down Barings Investment Bank in 1995 with losses of £850 million on futures and options trading. He tried to cover up his losses with lies and deceit. He was convicted of fraud and sentenced to six and a half years in jail in Singapore. John Rusnak worked with a subsidiary of Allied Irish Bank (AIB) in the US called Allfirst and made $691 million in losses in a similar situation to Nick Leeson. Similarly to Leeson, he used lies and deceit to cover up his losses. Rusnak was sentenced to seven and a half years in prison in 2003 after pleading guilty to a single count of bank fraud. He was ordered to pay $1,000 per month for five years when he finishes his sentence. Before his downfall, John was active in his local church and was a pillar of the local community.

Trust

Trust has been defined as the confidence in and reliance on good qualities especially fairness, truth, honour or ability. A person in a position of trust is expected by others to behave responsibly or honourably. In both business and life there can be no lasting relationships without trust. Trust is fragile. It can take years to earn, but can be lost in an instant.

In the Catholic and other churches clergymen broke their vows of celibacy and sexually abused young boys and girls. The situation was worsened by the obvious attempts to cover up the situation by the bishops. The bishops had no hesitation in telling lies to save the reputation of the church. In many instances they have lost the trust of their faithful. It will be extremely difficult to win back despite the excellent character of most priests in the church.

In business your word is your bond. Much business is still transacted through verbal agreements. Trust means when you say you'll do something, you'll do it and when you claim to know something, you know it. Without trust business cannot be transacted and sustained. Similarly, there can be no marriage without trust. When trust is gone the marriage disintegrates. Trustworthiness is a virtue universally accepted as a sign of good character and promotes good relationships. Although scepticism is healthy we must learn to trust others to get things done. Trust but verify should be your motto.

Destroying Trust

The following are some of the ways in which we can destroy trust:

- You say one thing and do another. We are trusted when we act in a consistent and truthful manner. There must be a positive relationship between words and deeds.

- You make promises you don't keep. In fact one gauge of a person's standard of ethics is the discrepancy between promises made and promises kept.

- You guard and selectively disclose information. In other words you are economical with the truth. Acts of omission can be just as unethical as acts of commission. Saying and doing nothing can be just as unethical as the committed act.

"Honesty is the cornerstone of all success, without which confidence and ability to perform shall cease to exist." — Mary Kay Ash

---

- You do what is expedient rather than what is right. You don't practise good ethics in all situations. You should not compromise your ethics even in seemingly insignificant situations, irrespective of the temptations. Dishonesty is a gradual process that begins with the bending of small rules. Every time we say or do something unethical, no matter how minor, we chip away at the foundations of our moral character and reputation.

- You put profits before people and Mammon before God.

- You are not authentic. You pretend to be something or somebody you are not. You put on a false mask. This means that the face you present to the world is not the real you. Trust comes from authenticity — we trust those whom we perceive to be genuine or credible.

- You manipulate people to achieve your own ends.

Summary

A personal code of ethics lays down the principles and values that will guide your conduct and behaviour throughout life. Values are precepts that we hold dear or believe to be intrinsically desirable. A good character is the foundation for a happy and successful life.

Character is about practising integrity, truth, honesty, sincerity, thoughtfulness, humility, kindness, good manners and compassion. Lack of integrity leads to fraud, corruption, bribery, dishonesty, forgery, greed, lies and deception. Lies and deceit have resulted in the downfall of many prominent politicians, business people and churchmen. They not only destroy their own lives but often those of their families and others as well.

Trust has been defined as the confidence in and reliance on good qualities, especially fairness, truth, honour or ability. There can be no lasting relationships without trust. Keeping your word oils the wheels of business and secures personal relationships. Corruption in the church has lost the trust of the faithful.

FIVE STEPS TO IMPROVING YOUR INTEGRITY

1. **Draw up a personal code of ethics setting down five things you should do to live an ethical life. Keep it somewhere visible as a constant reminder.**

2. **Reflect on what you mean by "character". What do you consider to be the essentials of a good character and how does your own character match up?**

3. **Name two US presidents who lied while in office. Reflect generally on the reasons why people lie.**

4. **Write down two reasons why honesty is always the best policy.**

5. **Consider why in business and in everyday life there can be no lasting relationships without trust. Write down two ways trust can be fostered.**

Case Study: Honesty is the Best Policy

George, who graduated with a good business degree, went to work after college in a large stockbroking firm in the city in which he grew up. He was very ambitious and hardworking and after 10 years was made a partner in the firm. In the meantime, George had married and was now the proud father of a daughter and son. Over the years George developed a secret gambling addiction. This eventually got so bad that he needed a lot of money to support his addiction. At first he won or broke even but eventually he made losses and ran up large debts. The people he owed money to threatened him with physical violence or worse if he did not pay his debts.

George started taking money from the business to pay his gambling debts and stave off the possibility of retribution towards him. At first the amounts were small and easy to cover up but as his addiction grew stronger the amounts stolen got larger. Clients who trusted George gave him money to buy shares on their behalf but instead he used the money to settle his gambling debts. He used forged documents to clients confirming the transactions even though they never took place. He also falsified the books and accounts of the firm to cover his tracks. In some instances he moved money between clients' accounts to cover up his shortfalls — a type of robbing Peter to pay Paul. George knew that it was only a matter of time before the scam was discovered.

The auditors arrived to do their annual audit and George was suffering from severe anxiety at the prospect of being found out. About a month into the audit they discovered the massive fraud which on further investigation they found went back a few years. George went out on sick leave, suffered from depression and attempted suicide. In the meantime the auditors had produced a sufficient case against George to ensure his conviction if brought to court. They discovered massive losses, to such an extent that the firm went bankrupt — its liabilities greatly exceeding its assets. There were insufficient funds to pay back the money lost by clients.

George was found guilty of falsifying books of accounts and records, of fraudulently converting clients' moneys to his own use and of obtaining funds under false pretences and was jailed for five years. His wife filed for divorce and for custody of the children and his parents and siblings refused to speak to him. His friends abandoned him. The firm closed down and 20 employees lost their jobs. Over 1,000 clients lost their savings and pension funds. Many were left practically destitute in their old age. George lost everything including his freedom and reputation. He will have plenty of time in jail to reflect on the misery he brought into his own life and the lives of others.

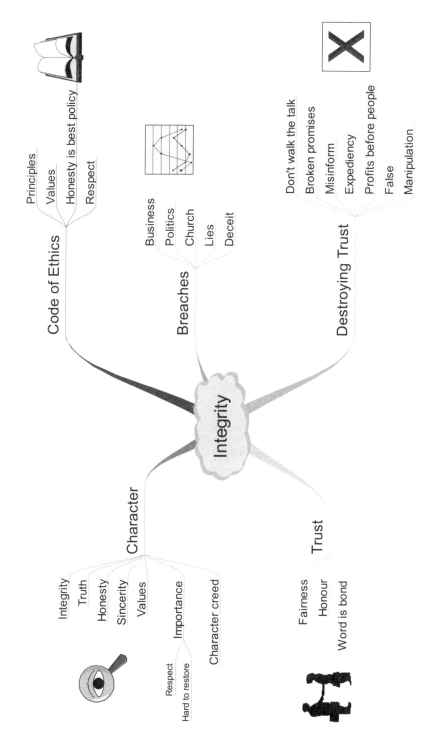

5

MOTIVATION

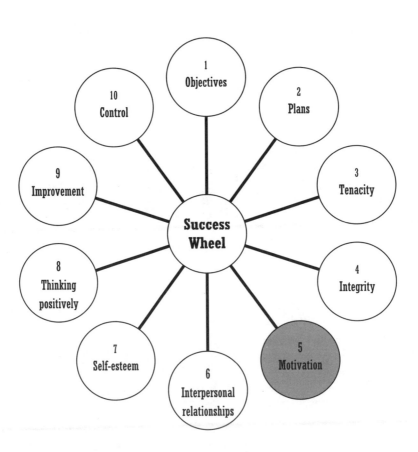

- ◆ What is motivation?
- ◆ What are the sources of motivation?
- ◆ What are drivers?
- ◆ Why is passion so important?
- ◆ What is the self-fulfilling prophecy?

"When we are motivated by goals that have deep meaning, by dreams that need completion, by pure love that needs expressing, then we truly live." — Greg Anderson

---

M is for motivation and is the fifth letter of our acronym OPTIMISTIC. Motivation has been defined as the force or process that impels people to behave in the way that they do. Without motivation nothing gets done and nobody succeeds in life. The sources of motivation can be internal or external. The drivers behind motivation are unique. Different things motivate different people. Hope, faith and passion are important drivers in motivation. The self-fulfilling prophecy suggests that what we expect is what we get. Our own expectations provide a positive motivational force. Those who expect to succeed at a task tend to be more successful than those who believe they will fail.

Source

The Latin root of the word "motivation" means to move. Motivation is therefore the study of action. Without motivation nothing gets done. There are two basic sources of motivation — internal and external. Internal motivation comes from within and is thus under your own control. Internally motivated people engage in activities because they are keenly interested and enthusiastic about them. Clear goals, vivid imagination, strong desire, a positive mental attitude and self-belief form the basis of internal motivation. For example, Leonardo da Vinci created his voluminous notebooks without any external prompting such as money or praise. It seems that people of genius are internally driven. They are pursuing their own personal goals which they self-regulate and self-monitor. They are driven by their own desires and needs rather than meeting the desires and needs of others. Achieving your own goals results in greater personal pride than achieving the goals set by others.

> **"What lies beyond us and what lies before us are tiny matters when compared to what lies within us" — Ralph Waldo Emerson**

Motivations derived from external sources include incentives, reinforcement and rewards. These may consist of money, bonuses, fringe benefits, praise, status or recognition. The drawback of relying on external rewards is that you are handing over responsibility for your motivation to others. This may diminish the strength of your own internal motivation. Externally motivated people may pursue an interest to be with friends or to enjoy being part of a group. A young person may study a particular degree programme just to please their parents or teachers. In a work context people are often motivated to do things to get the praise of their boss. Thus from the boss's perspective it is always better to praise and encourage rather than to criticise. A person never forgets an encouraging private word, when given with sincere respect and appreciation. As

Mother Teresa said, "There is more hunger for love and appreciation in this world than for bread."

Even envy may be a source of motivation. Carlin (2005) reports that Peter Salovey, Professor of Psychology at Yale, maintains that a mild dose of envy can energise and concentrate our efforts. He says, "If I really wish I had a car like my neighbour's, then that will motivate me to put my nose to the grindstone and earn more money in order to be able to buy that car." We are mainly concerned with our immediate reference group. If someone in your reference group has more than you, it may make you feel a bit uneasy and anxious. The reference group we compare ourselves with includes neighbours, siblings, relations, immediate work colleagues, former classmates and so on. This anxiety may motivate you to do something about it. It seems that peers in our little pond are the yardsticks of our own performance and sometimes the energisers of our motivation.

People may also be motivated to do something to experience pleasure, avoid pain or punishment while others may fear poverty, ignorance or losing their jobs. Optimistic and enthusiastic people are driven more towards the achievement of attractive goals rather than the need to avoid pain or punishment. Internally motivated people are more driven but we can benefit from external incentives as well. However, to be truly successful in life you need to be driven by your own needs. If you want to achieve something you must really want to do so for your own reasons and not for someone else's. Success in life is not about getting everything. Success is a matter of getting what you need.

Unique Drivers

We all possess basic physiological drivers such as the need for water and food, to have sex, to avoid pain and to maintain a stable temperature. For instance, food-seeking behaviour is motivated by hunger. However, the other drivers that motivate people are unique. People have unique ambitions, perspectives, beliefs, thoughts, attitudes, feelings and values. One person may value security while another likes risk and adventure. Some people are very ambitious while others like to casually watch the world go by. Some people are driven by the need for money and fame while others are driven by the need to help and serve others. Thus we have entrepreneurs who run our businesses and philanthropists and others who get involved with charities, social causes and politics.

"Be miserable. Or motivate yourself. Whatever has to be done, it's always your choice." — Wayne Dyer

---

One comprehensive theory of motivation was put forward by Maslow. He maintained that people had five needs, namely physical, safety, social, esteem and self-actualisation. As one need was met another took its place. In modern western society the first three needs are usually met by our jobs. The higher two needs are more difficult to meet. The highest need is self-actualisation which means reaching your potential in life by becoming what you are capable of becoming. Lifelong learning through continuous personal improvement and development would be one way of meeting this need. Our potential is unlimited and therefore the process of development should never end in our lifetime.

Hope

Hope is a constant motivator and keeps us going in the face of adversity, hardship and trauma throughout life. Hope is the belief that tomorrow will be better than today. Without hope we are only half-alive. With hope we dream, think, work and expect great things. Without any hope we would despair, stagnate and ultimately die.

Even those who are severely disabled have hopes for the future. Christopher Reeve, the actor who played the part of Superman, was totally paralysed from the neck down after a horse-riding accident in May 1995. However, right up to the time of his death he led an active life, acting, directing and writing though severely disabled and confined to a wheelchair. He appeared in a 1998 production of *Rear Window*, a modern version of the Alfred Hitchcock thriller about a man in a wheelchair who becomes convinced that a neighbour has been murdered. The role won him a Screen Actors Guild award. He never gave up hope that doctors would develop a way of regenerating the spinal cord in the future and that he would walk again some day. In 2000, he was able to move his index finger, and he maintained a strenuous workout regimen to make his limbs stronger. Reeve told the AP in an interview "I refuse to allow disability to determine how I live my life. I don't mean to be reckless, but setting a goal that seems a bit daunting actually is very helpful towards recovery." He lived by the mantra that nothing is impossible. However, it wasn't to be and he died in October 2004 at the age of 52 surrounded by his loving wife and family. He had become a passionate advocate for spinal cord research and a role model for those in similar circumstances. Future generations of those with spinal injuries will benefit from his work.

Physicist Stephen Hawking, who has motor neurone disease, can neither move nor speak yet his passion for life and science continues. In 1985 he contacted pneumonia and had to undergo a tracheotomy. This saved his life but took away his voice. He was given a computer system to enable him to have an electronic voice. He now needed 24-hour nursing care. Despite these difficulties he brought science to the layperson with the book *A Brief History of Time* which was an international best-seller when it was published in 1988. Despite his disability Stephen Hawking has never lost hope and continues his research into theoretical physics together with an extensive programme of travel and public lectures. In fact his renown as a scientist has increased as his disability has got worse. It's not what life hands you but your attitude and how you respond to it that's important. Hawking continues to combine his family life with his work. He is married with three children and a grandchild.

Without hope nothing would get done. The disabled would just despair and die. Entrepreneurs would not take risks if they did not hope to benefit in the future. People would not become self-employed without hope of achieving a better future. People would not emigrate in search of a better life. As J. Ollie Edmunds said, "This country was not built by men who relied on somebody else to take care of them. It was built by men who relied on themselves, who dared to shape their own lives, who had enough courage to blaze new trails — enough confidence in themselves to take the necessary risks".

Hope Eternal

Snyder (2002) describes how high hope people seek out alternative routes to their goals whereas low hope people are less flexible. High hope people are positive thinkers and tend to be confident whereas low hope people think negatively and lack confidence. The high hope person thinks in terms like "this should be interesting" or "I'm ready for this challenge". The low hope person thinks in terms like "This is too difficult" or "impossible". High hope people have a variety of goals and are capable of switching if an original goal proves unreachable. On the other hand, low hope people have fewer goals and are less adaptable. High hope people are less prone to stress than low hope people.

"Hope is a vigorous principle; it is furnished with light and heat to advise and execute; it sets the head and heart to work, and animates a man to do his utmost. And thus, by perpetually pushing and assurance, it puts a difficulty out of countenance, and makes a seeming impossibility give way." — Jeremy Collier

---

Most of us buy lottery tickets each week in the hope of winning a fortune. We know the odds of doing so are very low — one in several millions — but nevertheless our dreams persist. The expectation of the rewards of success in the long term will help us forgo the pleasures of short-term gratification in the present. Hope is strongest when obstacles are perceived as not being insurmountable. However, hope should be tempered with good reason, realism and judgement.

To help us develop a positive approach we should reframe obstacles as challenges to be overcome or opportunities to be exploited. Self-belief such as affirming "I can do this" and "I'm not going to be stopped" creates the right sense of determination and expectation. On successful completion of a task our self-confidence is reinforced. Success begets success and increases our sense of self-efficacy. On the other hand, lack of confidence multiplies with failures.

Expectation

People rise to their own expectations and the expectations of significant others. Expectations that are set too low mean that you are not living up to your potential. Expectations that are set too high set us up for failure and disappointment. Maintain high but attainable expectations for yourself and then inspire yourself on to achieve them. High and seemingly impossible expectations sometimes become the norm.

Decades ago, many people thought it was impossible to run a mile in under four minutes. Medical experts maintained that the human heart would burst under the strain. However, Roger Bannister didn't believe this and broke the four-minute barrier in 1954. Within months many others had also broken the four-minute barrier and since then thousands of runners have done so. Before 1954 many runners were capable of breaking the four-minute barrier. The only thing stopping them was their lack of belief. Once we believe something is possible, we somehow become capable of doing it.

"The vast majority of people are born, grow up, struggle, and go through life in misery and failure, not realising that it would be just as easy to switch over and get exactly what they want out of life, not recognising that the mind attracts that thing it dwells upon." — Dr Napoleon Hill

---

Psychologists have found that a person's positive image of the future may be a better predictor of future attainment than past performance. The strongest motivator is when you really believe that you will achieve your goals. The mind moves towards your current dominant thought. The mind believes and does what it is consistently told. Therefore you have the power to move in any direction that you choose.

You are totally responsible for and have total control over your own thoughts. Make sure these thoughts are positive, constructive, happy, self-affirming and directed towards worthwhile goals. Beliefs act as self-fulfilling prophecies. If you act as if what you desire is possible then you will do what is necessary to bring about the result.

What You See is What You Get

You are limited to a large extent by your own expectations, perceptions, beliefs, hopes and fears. If you have low expectations for yourself you will never achieve much. Expect the best and the best is more likely to happen. You see and get what you look for in life. Your attitudes project what you see. Hold yourself in high regard and others will be encouraged to do likewise. See yourself as a high achiever and your expectations are more likely to be realised. See yourself as a failure and others will treat you like one.

> **"Strong lives are motivated by dynamic purposes; lesser ones exist on wishes and inclinations." — Kenneth Hildebrand**

Everybody has problems. Nobody escapes the normal ups and downs of life. Don't expect to be happy all the time. You must be able to live with the bad times as well as the good. Adopt a solution-centred approach to life rather than a problem-centred one. See problems as challenges and opportunities and try to see the positive side to life's trials and tribulations. Review your experiences and learn to go forward with a positive frame of mind.

The Pygmalion Effect

The Pygmalion Effect suggests that in addition to our own expectations we also are influenced by the expectations of significant others. In experiments, students were found to live up to the high expectations of their teachers. In a work context it has been found that workers are influenced by the high expectations of their supervisors and managers. In our formative and early years our parents and peer group have a major influence on our behaviour. Our behaviour is often determined by the expectations of our parents.

Our conditioning is deep-rooted, firstly by our parents and then by our peer group. Constant negative criticism may become a self-fulfilling prophecy. If children are constantly told they are worthless they may come to believe that eventually and achieve little in life. Similarly, people who hear nothing but criticism inevitably feel inadequate and resentful. On the other hand, if their achievements are constantly affirmed and nurtured they may go on to achieve great things.

The Placebo Effect

In medicine there is a well-know phenomenon known as the placebo effect. This is where people are given a harmless substance instead of real medicine. Nevertheless many of them get better. It is a question of faith conquering all. People who have intense faith in their doctors and believe they will get well are highly motivated to do so and often recover beyond the expectations of their physicians. It seems to be a case of mind over matter. Expectation undoubtedly makes an important contribution to the placebo effect. Across a wide range of illnesses, patients who expect to improve are more likely to improve.

Brown (1997) reports that expectation operates more specifically as well. For example, when people were given an alcohol-free drink but told that it contained alcohol, they often felt intoxicated, and some showed some of the physical signs of intoxication. In another study, when people with asthma were given an inhaler containing only salt-water and told that they would be inhaling an irritant or allergen, they reported increased airway obstruction and had more difficulty breathing. But when told that the same inhaler had a medicine to help asthma, their airways opened up and they breathed more easily. Many diseases, such as the common cold, improve without intervention. So some patients who get better with placebo treatment — and some who get better with standard treatment — would have got better if left to themselves.

Faith healing, which customarily involves touching, is based on trust and belief and sometimes results in "miracle" cures. These cures may be the result of the placebo effect. On the other hand, the power of belief can also be a negative motivational force. In the voodoo religion a curse from a witch doctor may prove fatal for the victim. Members of the tribe who have a death spell cast upon them die within a few days.

Passion

Having passion means that you are doing the things you really want to do and that you are doing the things that make you feel most alive and inspired. People with passion are animated, enthused and committed. Being committed means that you will do whatever it takes to achieve your goals. Some of our great inventions were inspired by perceived needs. For example, Dr Edwin Land's daughter, who couldn't understand why it took so long to develop pictures, inspired him to invent instant photography. Bill Gates, the founder of Microsoft Corporation, was inspired by the vision to make computing power available to the masses. Similarly, Henry Ford wanted to produce a car that anybody could afford.

> **"There is no greatness without a passion to be great, whether it's the aspiration of an athlete or an artist, a scientist, a parent, or a businessperson." — Tony Robbins**

Feeling frustrated or even angry about something often provides the motivation for great deeds. Some of the founders of the great charities and social movements throughout history were motivated by a sense of vocation, anger at injustices or poverty seen, compassion and a deep desire to put things right and make the world a better place. Ambitious people are usually passionate about their subject or cause. Ambition and passion fires drive. Without ambition and passion the smartest person may achieve little in life. It is the doers and risk takers and those who learn from their experience who reap the rewards of life. Martin Luther King, Mother Teresa and Albert Schweitzer led very inspirational lives and they should act as an example to the rest of us.

Passionate People

Martin Luther King had a dream of the USA being free from racial prejudice, discrimination, segregation and injustice. He was inspired by the methods of Gandhi and used non-violent protest to achieve his aims. Even though it is still a work-in-progress most of his goals have been realised. His speech "I have a dream . . . that all men are created equal" is probably one of the most passionate speeches of all time. Following the Civil Rights Act of 1964, which helped to end discrimination against Blacks in the USA, King was awarded the Nobel Peace Prize. Later on in his career he took on the cause of the poor and downtrodden of America. He once said, "If a man hasn't discovered something he's willing to die for, he isn't fit to live". This proved to be prophetic. On 4 April 1968 he was assassinated. His birthday, 15 January, is now a national holiday in the USA.

"A strong passion for any object will ensure success, for the desire of the end will point out the means." — Henry Hazlitt

---

Mother Teresa is now revered throughout the world for her unshakeable sense of purpose and passion to help the poor and dying of Calcutta whose plight touched her heart deeply. She is now a candidate for sainthood. Faith, hope and charity were the driving forces in her life. Her total faith in God inspired her to found the Order of Missionaries of Charity who continue to do her work to this day. This organisation now helps the poor and rejected in 123 countries throughout the world. Her faith was reinforced by her hope in expectation of salvation in Heaven and her belief in the tenet, "Love God and thy neighbour as thyself." Mother Teresa said: "Yesterday is gone and tomorrow has not yet come, so we must live each day as if it were our last so that when God calls us we are ready, and prepared to die with a clean heart."

Albert Schweitzer, philosopher, physician and humanitarian, has been called the greatest Christian of all time. He based his personal philosophy on reverence for life and on a deep commitment to serve humanity. He abandoned a promising career as a musician and theologian to fulfil his ambition to serve the needs of others. For his many years of humanitarian efforts he was awarded the Nobel Peace Prize in 1962. Schweitzer was inspired to become a medical missionary after reading an evangelical paper about the needs of medical missions. He built a hospital in French Equatorial Africa serving thousands of Africans. He used his $33,000 Nobel Prize, royalties from books and fees for personal appearances to expand the hospital and to build a leper colony. In 1955 Queen Elizabeth II awarded him the "Order of Merit", Britain's highest civilian honour.

How to Motivate Yourself

- Be genuinely enthusiastic, interested and committed in whatever you do. Without enthusiasm, passion and an inherent interest in a topic there is unlikely to be lasting motivation. Interest alone and emotional investment can take you far on the road to success. Nothing great was ever achieved without enthusiasm. But enthusiasm combined with doing what you love is intrinsically motivational.

"Everyone is enthusiastic at times. One person has enthusiasm for 30 minutes, another for 30 days, but it is the one who has it for 30 years who makes a success in life."— Edward B. Butler

---

- Perception. Anticipating the outcome as positive, pleasurable and desirable obviously increases the intensity of the motivation we experience. On the other hand, seeing something as negative, painful or frightening will have a negative motivational impact. For example, Sigmund Freud proposed the pleasure principle as the primary source of motivation. He said that people are driven to seek pleasure and avoid pain.

- Take responsibility for your own emotions and behaviour. To be emotionally responsible means that you accept that you create your own feelings in reaction to life issues. You don't blame other people such as your parents, manager or partner for how you feel. Behavioural responsibility means that you control your own reactions and behaviours, and are not compelled to behave in any particular way. You refuse to be a victim and over-react to what other people do or say. Remember, God helps those who help themselves. Other people have their own needs that they put first and these may not correspond with yours. The more you feel in control of your life the more likely you are to be successful. After all, you are the chief executive of your own destiny.

- Identify what motivates you. Different things motivate different people. Some people want fame or fortune, more want leisure time, opportunities to travel, own a nice house, a nice car or a combination of these. Others want praise or recognition, or love and acceptance. What do you want? Success should be a means to an end — to get what you really want. The desire to contribute to society, to make a difference, to grow and develop, and to leave a legacy are some of the things that motivate most people. Whatever motivates you, do things for your own reasons.

- Provide yourself with a challenge. This means setting goals and targets that are stretching but achievable. Continuous goal-setting throughout your life means you are always challenged since you have always one more rung of the ladder to climb or one more goal to achieve.

- Welcome difficulty. Successful people want an interesting life rather than an easy one. Solving complex and difficult problems is stimulating and motivational.

- Learn new things. Provide extra challenge for yourself by undertaking new courses of study or reading new subject areas from time to time. Reading exercises your memory and imagination and provides food for a positive mental attitude. By constantly raising the bar and learning new things you create a challenge, interest and at the same time avoid boredom. Learning essential worthwhile skills, challenged and driven by curiosity and interest, is intrinsically motivational.

- Recognise your accomplishments by celebrating them. This should be done during the process as well as at the end. Don't wait around for other people to praise you. Affirm and praise yourself. You may think that self-praise is no praise but it is motivational.

**"Motivation will almost always beat mere talent."
— Norman R. Augustine**

- Be creative. There seems to be a natural hunger in human beings to pursue challenges by seeking out the unusual, solve problems, innovate and exploit your creativity to the best of your ability. Creativity is usually an expression of a genuine interest in a problem rather than a consequence of monetary incentive. We are all endowed with powers of creative imagination that we can develop by taking an interest in our surroundings. It just means that we should take every opportunity to exploit our curiosity and natural powers of ingenuity.

- Become part of a group with similar interests. Enthusiasm is contagious and so you are sure to benefit from others' interests and also learn from each other.

- Enjoy the path or process to achieving your goals. Have fun and keep a sense of humour. The journey should be just as rewarding or even more rewarding as reaching the destination. Educate yourself about the process. Knowing more about the process means you are more efficient and have more control over it.

- Realise there is no failure, only feedback. Most of us welcome positive feedback but find it difficult to accept negative feedback. Welcome any feedback and learn to react positively to negative feedback. Have an open mind. Unless you are able to learn and improve you will never benefit from your mistakes. Have plenty of targets on the way to your goal as small successes enhance motivation and keep you on track. The habit of success becomes ingrained and is laid down as patterns in your brain thus ensuring further success. There is truth in the saying, "Nothing succeeds like success."

- Look ahead to future possibilities of continued accomplishments rather than looking behind with regrets at failed attempts. The past is gone and the same opportunity will never be repeated. The past is not the future. Move on by acknowledging what went wrong and learning from the experience and stride towards making the next decision more positive and productive.

Summary

Without motivation nothing gets done. There are two sources of motivation, namely internal and external. Internal motivators are best since they are self-determined and self-regulated. Drivers are the unique ambitions, perspectives, beliefs, thoughts, attitudes, feelings and values compelling people forward towards their goals.

Hope is a constant motivator and keeps us going in the face of adversity, hardship, and trauma throughout our lives. Hope is the belief that tomorrow will be better than today.

People rise to their own high expectations and the expectations of significant others. In psychology this is known as the self-fulfilling prophecy and the Pygmalion Effect. Self-belief is an important ingredient of success.

Passion means that you are doing the things you really want to do and that you are doing the things that make you feel most excited and alive. People with passion are inspired, enthused and committed.

FIVE STEPS TO IMPROVING YOUR MOTIVATION

1. **Reflect on the difference between internal and external motivation. Write down the reasons why internal motivation is more effective than external motivation.**

2. **Reflect on the unique ambitions you have for your life. Write down the concrete actions necessary to achieve them and then set in motion an implementation plan.**

3. **Consider whether or not you have high expectations for yourself about what you should achieve in life. Why are your own expectations and those of others significant motivators?**

4. **Passion is an important motivator. Write down two things in life you feel very passionate about and consider how these might be transformed into a motivational career or life goal.**

5. **Write down four ways to motivate yourself. Actively incorporate these into your mindset and behaviours.**

Case Study: Motivation

Paula had always harboured the ambition to write a non-fiction book. She was fifty years old and had taken early retirement recently. She had previously been employed as a college lecturer in management studies. Over the years she had accumulated an encyclopaedic knowledge of management through her extensive reading, lecturing and research. She had always had a particular interest in how students learn and the best way to facilitate the process. In fact she had often run one-day workshops in study skills and examination technique for her students. However, up to now she had never seemed to have the time to write a book.

Earlier attempts to write had been procrastinated and eventually abandoned. She had become discouraged when confronted with obstacles and hated making the inevitable mistakes. She knew that getting a book published could be difficult and imagined she would find it hard to cope with the inevitable rejection slips from publishers. In addition, she always seemed to be too busy and other things always got priority. She was now confident that she would commit the necessary time and resources to see the project through from start to finish.

She wanted to write a book on study skills for the student market. In the past she had used mind maps as a technique for researching her lectures, as a way of summarising chapters in textbooks and as a presentation technique for delivering lectures. She now intended to use them as a way of researching, brainstorming and planning the various chapters for the proposed book. She also thought about the principles of motivation, such as planning, chunking and setting objectives and how she might use them to motivate herself to write her book.

Chunking is a method of breaking down a task into manageable components. Writing a book naturally lends itself to this idea as each chapter is a "chunk" of a book and each section of a chapter is a "chunk" of a chapter. She decided she would have ten chapters in the book, each chapter covering a study skills topic such as time management, memory skills, mind mapping, presentation and examination technique. The number of sections within a chapter would vary but on average would be about ten. She would summarise each chapter in mind map form and she bought a mind map software package to design and draw the mind maps. The final draft of these mind map summaries would be incorporated with the manuscript as chapter summaries.

Paula estimated that the planning stage and research for the book would take two months and that each chapter should take a month to write. One week of each month would be devoted to editing and improving the text and three weeks would be devoted to the actual writing of the chapter. Her target was to write at least one page per day. She estimated that the book would be about 120 pages in length. The book would be aimed at business students and when writing she kept this continually in the forefront of her mind.

She also kept in mind all the time that a journey of 120 pages begins with a single page. From the start she visualised a successful outcome and saw in her mind's eye the finished product on the bookshops' shelves. She was determined that this time she would stick to the task and see it through to completion. She realised that most of the fun in writing is in the process and that this high-lights the importance of targets to be reached on the way to the finishing line. During the process she used positive self-talk and affirmations and celebrated the achievement of significant stages. Doing this helped her to stay motivated and focused on her goals. Affirmations alone are of little value. They must be accompanied by appropriate action. Internally motivated desire rather than ex-ternal reward mainly motivate the writing of a book.

Paula allocated six hours per day to the task of writing the book. She started each morning at 8.00 am and worked through until 12.30 pm, with a half-hour break for coffee at 10.45 am. In the afternoon she worked between 2.00 pm and 4.00 pm. She did this routine from Monday to Thursday. The rest of the week she used for other pursuits and as leisure time. It was important to get down to the task as nothing gets done until you actually start. She found that having started the book it created its own momentum and the monthly "chunks" and targets created their own goals. She realised that she would meet obstacles and make mistakes on the way to her goals but treated these as challenges and learning opportunities.

On target, Paula completed her manuscript in one year. She now had the task of getting a publisher. She was a member of a professional accountancy body with a student membership of 60,000. This accountancy body had a publications division and she knew that they did not have a study skills book for their stu-dents. She rang the publisher and was surprised to hear that they were currently looking for an author to write such a book. She told them she had a manuscript prepared and they informed her that they would be interested in seeing such a book with a view to publication. Within a month the editor was back with some sug-gestions about making the book more focused on their student market. Paula took the suggestions on board and within another month had returned the amended manuscript. Within three months the book was published and has become one of the Institute's best sellers. Paula is aware that publishers reject nine out of ten manu-scripts and so she is naturally very proud of her achievement in be-coming a published author. She now has the incentive to write a second book and she has already started thinking about her next topic.

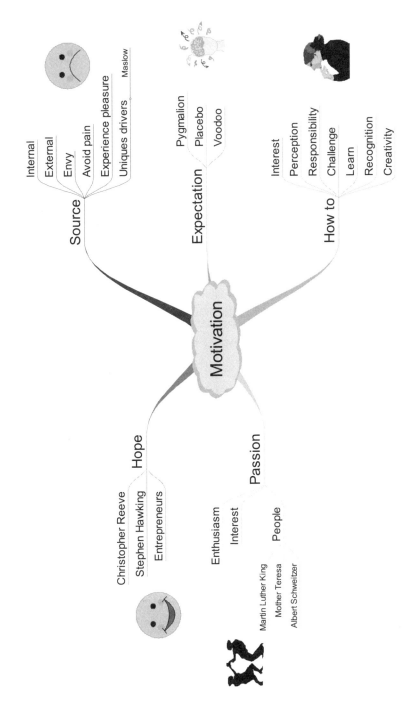

6

INTERPERSONAL RELATIONSHIPS

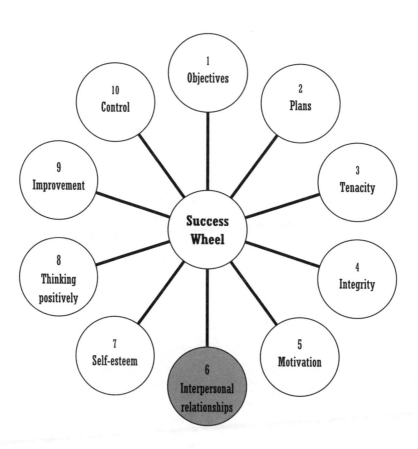

- ♦ What are the secrets of being popular?
- ♦ Why are good relationships so important to success?
- ♦ How can I improve my communication skills?
- ♦ What is assertiveness?
- ♦ How can I overcome shyness?

"The ability to form friendships, to make people believe in you and trust you is one of the few absolutely fundamental qualities of success. Selling, buying, negotiating are so much smoother and easier when the parties enjoy each other's confidence. The young man who can make friends quickly will find that he will glide instead of stumble through life." — John J. McGuirk

---

I stands for interpersonal relationships and is the sixth letter in our acronym OPTIMISTIC. Practising good interpersonal relationships is an important ingredient in our success model. It is the quality of our relationships that ultimately determine our success in life. Popular people show appreciation for others and practise good social skills. They focus on the needs of the other person rather than their own.

People with good interpersonal relationship skills are able to empathise and communicate effectively with others. Networking with others is a great way of making contacts, developing friendships and sharing expertise. Assertiveness is an essential skill to develop if you want to be taken seriously. Shy people are self-conscious and worry what others think about them. There are many ways of overcoming shyness, including learning how to relax and getting involved socially with others.

Popular People

Popular people know how to relate effectively with others. Somebody once said that it was nice to be important but it was more important to be nice. Popular people think positively by always looking for and focusing on the good points in others. They know that people crave appreciation and so they respect and value the uniqueness of others. Deep down we all just want our distinctiveness to be acknowledged. Popular people treat others as they would like others to treat them. They are prepared to show kindness by helping others in small ways. They realise if they help others to meet their needs they will feel good about themselves and are most likely to be helped in return. They look for the talent in others and encourage them to use it and develop it further.

Popular people say what they mean and mean what they say. Their word is their bond and they follow through on their commitments. Nothing kills relationships more than people who fail to keep their promises.

"He liked to like people, therefore people liked him."
— Mark Twain

Popular people are socially aware and have good social skills. They exude confidence by their speech, dress, posture and behaviour. They think before they speak and are sensitive to the feelings of others. They make people feel valued, capable, loved, respected and appreciated. They know how to read people and situations. They try to inspire rather than antagonise others. If they feel compelled to admonish others they criticise the behaviour rather than the person. They are good at reconciling different perspectives and winning commitment. They realise that they need to be flexible in their dealings with others. It is often the case of having different strokes for different folks. They know how to influence, collaborate and cooperate with others to meet mutually agreed aims.

On the other hand, socially inept people cause others to feel devalued, inadequate, undermined, angry, resentful, frustrated or guilty. Socially inept people have little or no insight or empathy into the relationship needs of others. They are often condescending, arrogant, abrasive, belligerent and insensitive. They are so preoccupied with their own lives and needs that they are completely unaware of the impact they have on others. As a result they make enemies instead of friends as they go through life. This is counterproductive as confirmed by the old saying, "Friends come and go but enemies accumulate."

IQ + EQ = Success

Popular people are emotionally competent. They realise that IQ + EQ = Success. In other words, you need to combine your conventional intelligence with emotional intelligence to be successful. Part of emotional intelligence is self-understanding and understanding the needs of others. It is very difficult to understand others if you don't understand yourself. Self-awareness is at the core of developing social skills. You may think you know who you are but you might be surprised how other people perceive you. Seek out feedback from others who you can rely on to be sincere. Use the feedback to improve your self-understanding and social skills.

The map is not the territory, so the way you perceive the world is not how the world really is. You filter the world through your own eyes influenced by your unique culture, experience, expectations, education, attitudes, beliefs and values. Other people do likewise, so that everybody has a different perception of the world. This highlights why it is so difficult to empathise or be sensitive to the fears, feelings and concerns of others. Empathy is the ability to connect with others and see things from their point of view. Empathy is easy to talk about but very difficult to practise.

Popular people know how to make friends and try to choose friends with similar values. It seems the old adage, that birds of a feather stick together, is true. However, when differences occur they know how to handle rejections, disagreements and conflict. Disagreeing with someone produces a 60 per cent chance that they will disagree back. It's better to probe and understand their point of view. They know how to defuse, resolve and practise conflict management skills. Socially confident people stop conflict from escalating. They apologise, make a peace offering of some kind, change the subject, or negotiate a mutually acceptable solution. It's very hard to argue with someone who doesn't argue back. Managing conflict without aggression requires collaboration, listening, understanding the perspectives of others, controlling negative emotions, and working out creative solutions to problems.

Humour used appropriately can be employed to deflect and defuse tense situations. So develop a sense of humour and enjoy your interactions with others. Humour has many benefits. We now know that humour stimulates various brain centres, raises pain tolerance, strengthens the immune system and is an antidote to stress.

Difference between SI and EI

Social intelligence has been defined as the ability to get along and co-operate with others. It is a combination of social skills, self-awareness and interaction style. Albrecht (2004) makes a distinction between social intelligence and emotional intelligence and illustrates the point with reference to the late President Ronald Reagan of the USA. Ronald Reagan, while President, won the love and affection of many Americans and indeed many people throughout the world. On his visit to Ireland, the home of his ancestors, he won the affection of the Irish people by his outgoing personality and obvious charisma. When he left office and he developed Alzheimer's disease, the sense of affection towards him grew even more. After his death, his funeral evoked an outpouring of grief and admiration. Most of the American media presented him as a loveable father figure and compassionate leader. However, some opponents of his politics were amazed at the way he was elevated to the stature of heroic leader.

Many observers found a contradiction between his emotional and social personas. In his public life, Reagan was able to charm people individually and collectively. Nevertheless, he was a man whom very few people knew well or connected with on a deeply personal level. His relationships with close family members were generally distant and strained. People who worked closely with him on a daily basis reported that he showed very little personal interest in them. One of his biographers reported that Reagan used the same stories many times, told in exactly the same way, with the same words, the same voice cadence, pauses, gestures and facial expressions. Reagan was indubitably the supreme actor.

Based on these observations, it seems reasonable to characterise Reagan as a man of remarkably high social intelligence but low emotional intelligence. Reagan was good at relating to people on a superficial social level but was unable to do so on a personal emotional basis. Therefore while social intelligence and emotional intelligence are connected, they are not exactly the same. Emotional intelligence involves a meeting of hearts and minds.

Communication Skills

To relate effectively with others we must talk to them in a friendly and sincere way. Conversation is about exchanging information, thoughts, concerns, feelings, ideas, courtesies, pleasantries, greetings and compliments. We all have a tendency to pack in as many words in a sentence as we can. However, good speakers speak more slowly than others. The faster you speak the less likely you are to be understood. Peterson et al. (1995) found that speakers who speak more slowly are perceived as being 38 per cent more knowledgeable than speakers who speak more quickly.

Think before you speak and about the likely consequences of what you are going to say. This will prevent us from making fools of ourselves or hurting the feelings of others. Be polite and use the common courtesies such as "Please", "Thank you" and

"Excuse me". It is surprising how many people fail to do this. We should be able to receive and make compliments. These are the little things that oil the wheels of conversation and help to make daily living a more pleasant experience. Get the other person's name and use it occasionally during the conversation. People love to hear the sound of their own name.

"Communication leads to community, that is, to under-standing, intimacy and mutual valuing . . ." — **Rollo May**

Be sincere. People trust and confide in others who are genuine and keep their promises. We also trust people who tell the truth even if we don't like what they're saying. However, in reality you should realise that words and behaviour are not always consistent. People often say one thing and do another. The most reliable guide to behaviour is what people do rather than what they say.

Listening

When engaged in conversation we should listen twice as much as we speak. Somebody once said that this is the reason why we have two ears and one mouth. Most people are more interested in themselves and what they have to say than in you and what you have to say. That's why the most popular people are good listeners. The best way to build up rapport with people is to listen and be actively interested in what they have to say. Be curious about other people, what they think, what they feel and what they say. People just want somebody to listen to their concerns and troubles — a friendly ear to confide in. Hence the reason why people are prepared to pay large fees to psycho-therapists and counsellors to listen to them.

While listening we should really do so rather than spend the time thinking up what we are going to say next. It is difficult to think and listen at the same time. Many people cut across others while speaking and thus spoil any rapport built up between them. The average person speaks at the rate of about 125 to 165 words per minute. We think at about four times that rate. Therefore, you have abundant capacity for distraction if you fail to concentrate on what the other person is saying. Genuinely listening to other people increases the likelihood that they will return the compliment.

"I like to listen. I have learned a great deal from listening carefully. Most people never listen." — Ernest Hemingway

---

Paraphrase occasionally what the other person is saying and reflect back the feelings as well as the content of the message. This will help to keep you both on the same wavelength. Remember, communication does not take place until it is understood. Communication consists of three elements: a sender, a message and a receiver. There are all sorts of reasons why communication may go wrong. The sender may not use appropriate words, the transmission system may distort the message, and the receiver may misunderstand the words. In addition, our beliefs and attitudes affect how we interpret the message.

Mirroring is a technique where you occasionally reflect back exactly what the speaker is saying like a tape recorder. It doesn't mean that you agree with what the speaker is saying. It just means that you are confirming back what is said. It slows down the pace and allows people to reflect on the content of the conversation. Try to understand rather than judge. If you suggest things rather than dogmatically insisting you will find that agreement is more forthcoming. The harder you push people, the harder they will resist. You can also mirror body language such as gestures and posture. Mirroring body language and speech patterns is a good way of building rapport. However, this should be done in a subtle way without any hint of mimicry.

Avoid Formal Language

Avoid the use of formal language such as "it has been brought to my attention" and parental language such as "can't", "must", "should" and "ought". These autocratic words remind you of what your parents used to say to you as a child and consequently irritate and increase resistance. Communicate with people at their own level. Clarity is the ability to express one-self clearly, use words effectively, explain difficult concepts simply and persuade others with logical argument. This can be summarised in the KISS technique: Keep It Simple and Straight-forward.

Use open-ended questions beginning with what? why? when? where? how? and who? to elicit information and keep the conversation going. Try to get to know others well. Show an interest in their hobbies, work and family. As part of the listening process observe body language. Gestures, tone of voice and facial expressions are important in understanding what some-one is saying. Surreptitiously match the body language and voice tone of others to build up rapport.

Smile

Keep in touch with friends to maintain and nurture relation-ships. We need social support systems to remain psychologi-cally healthy. Sharing information and expertise and giving and asking for help as appropriate will cement relationships and make life worthwhile.

Of all the things you wear, your expression is the most im-portant. Learn to smile naturally. A smile says, "I like you and find you pleasant company". A smile costs nothing but is the most valuable thing you can give to others. The entertainer, Victor Borge, said a smile was the shortest distance between two people. A pleasant disposition attracts people while an un-pleasant one discourages interactions with others.

Making an Impression

The acronym SIMPLE will help you remember some of the things we have discussed and what you need to do to make a good impression:

- **S**peech. Develop a friendly and pleasant tone of voice. Vary the tone of your speaking voice to create variety and ex-citement. It is very difficult to listen to somebody who speaks in a monotonous tone. Give emphasis as appropri-ate. You can increase the volume of your voice for certain key words to emphasise their importance. Vary the speed of your speech. Speeding up creates excitement while a slower speed creates calm and reflection. Intimacy may be created by a low voice. Avoid filler words such as "you know", "basically" and "like". These add nothing to meaning and may be a source of annoyance to your listener.

- Involve your listener. Conversation should be a two-way process rather than a monologue. If you monopolise a conversation you are sure to be considered a bore. Make sure you listen more than you speak. You never learn while you're talking. Use your sense of curiosity. Get the other person involved by asking appropriate questions. Solicit opinions. Find the common ground. Ask them about their likes and dislikes. Everybody is an expert on something. Use good follow-up questions. Using the word "why?" now and then is sure to keep the conversation going. Also use "what if?" questions as appropriate. These should be logical extensions to the questions asked. People love to talk about themselves. On the other hand, the best way to stop a conversation is to belittle or put a person down. Smile! A smile puts people at their ease. A good conversationalist will do everything possible to get the shyest person in the group involved.

- Mirror body language. Do this unobtrusively. This creates the impression that you are in harmony with the other person. Also mirror their language to show you are on the same wavelength. Remember, body language is a natural part of communication.

- Positive handshake. When meeting somebody a firm handshake creates the impression that you are confident and interested. A weak handshake may indicate lack of confidence or lack of interest. Notice the way good politicians radiate confidence, warmth and interest by the two-arm handshake. While shaking hands they lightly grab the person's arm with their left hand while shaking hands with the right.

- Lean forward. This shows that you are interested in what they are saying. Leaning backwards creates the impression that your are bored and want to disengage.

- **E**ye contact. Make frequent eye contact. Don't stare. Eye contact should last about two to three seconds each time. Give the person your total attention to make them feel that they are the most important person in the room. Staring vaguely into space or looking over the person's shoulder to see who else is in the room does not display interest. However, when you're talking you may take your eyes off your partner occasionally.

Assertiveness

To succeed in life you need to be able to fight your own battles and speak with conviction. The following has been adapted from Malone (1999). There is a difference between being passive, aggressive and assertive. Being passive or non-assertive means:

- Having difficulty standing up for oneself. Letting people "walk all over you". You are not a doormat.

- Voluntarily giving up responsibility for yourself and handing it over to others who may not have your true interests at heart. They certainly are unlikely to put your interests ahead of their own.

- Encouraging persecution by assuming the role of victim or martyr. In transactional analysis, this is known as the game "kick me": manipulating others into hurting or punishing you.

> **"The basic difference between being assertive and being aggressive is how our words and behavior affect the rights and well-being of others." — Sharon Anthony Bower**

Being aggressive means:

- Standing up for your rights in such a way that others' rights and feelings are violated.

- Being self-enhancing at the expense of others by putting them down or humiliating them. This may include using past wrongs, imagined or real, as an excuse to hurt another.

- Antagonising others by hostile or offensive words or deeds.

On the other hand, assertiveness means being able to express your needs, preferences and feelings in a way that is neither abrasive, threatening, unmannerly nor harmful to others:

- Without causing undue annoyance, fear or anxiety.

- Without violating the rights of others.

- Without demeaning the value of others.

Assertiveness means direct, honest communication between individuals interacting equally and taking responsibility for themselves. Assertiveness is about choice and having respect for yourself without losing respect for others. Unfortunately, double standards often operate; for example, women who are assertive are often seen as pushy, aggressive and unfeminine, while assertiveness in men is seen as a sign of strength and confidence.

My Bill of Rights

This is a well-known charter for people who want to be assertive. It is based on democratic principles. I have the right to:

- State my own needs and accept that they are as important as anybody else's.

- Be treated with respect and respect others likewise.

- Express my feelings with conviction in a composed but confident way but with consideration for others.

- Have and give my own opinions.

- Stick to my point. If necessary repeat it calmly and politely until I get my point of view across.

- Say "yes" or "no" as appropriate.

- Set my own priorities.

- State the personal difficulties that others' requests will cause.

- Ask for "thinking over time" as necessary.

- Make mistakes. After all nobody is perfect and people do learn from their mistakes.

- Change my mind. This is not a sign of weakness but sensible in certain circumstances.

- Say that I don't know or don't understand. Nobody knows everything.

- Ask for what I want. If you don't ask you have no chance of receiving.

- Refuse to take responsibility for the problems of others. You are only responsible for your own feelings and responses.

- Deal with others without being dependent on them for approval.

- Run my own life and take responsibility for my actions.

- Take pride in my successes without being pompous or arrogant.

- Stand up for my rights without violating the rights of others.

Basic Assertiveness Skills

There are many assertiveness skills available. The following are four of the most popular:

- **"Broken record"**. This is one of the most widely used assertiveness techniques. It is called the "broken record" because when a record gets stuck in a grove, it plays the same thing over and over. Similarly, you repeat the same thing over and over until your point has been accepted or your wishes conceded. This technique will enable you to stick by your decision when confronted with bullying, an overbearing person, or manipulation. It will also help you deal with authority figures in a confident and assertive manner.

- **Saying "No"**. Many people are reluctant or find it very difficult to say "No". Some find it difficult to say "No" to those in authority; others may be afraid of the aggressive response that a "No" might elicit. Remember, you have a right to say "No" and that saying "No" is much better than agreeing to do something that you do not want to do and subsequently letting people down. Give the reason for refusing. Don't invent excuses. It is not necessary to apologise profusely, if at all. If appropriate, suggest an alternative.

- **"Fogging"**. "Fogging" allows you to be criticised without becoming defensive, anxious or argumentative while, at the same time, preventing the other person from manipulating you. It defuses a potentially acrimonious situation from developing. If someone says something to provoke you, "Fogging" slows the tempo down and calms the atmosphere by deflection. You side-step the issue, while still retaining your composure and point of view, by partly agreeing with what they say. For example, if the boss says, "That was a stupid proposal you put forward at the meeting", you might say, "Yes, I can see that you think my proposal was foolish". You are not agreeing with your boss; you are only saying that you can see that they believe that.

- **The "ALL" technique.** Alexander (2004) reports that the "ALL" technique may be useful in appropriate situations. "A" stands for acknowledgement. "L" stands for the list of things you need to do. The second "L" stands for listing alternatives. For example, say your manager has approached you late on Thursday with a request to do a very urgent project that would entail you working late. You should acknowledge that the project is very important to the manager. You should then make the manager aware of the current projects that you are doing. Tell him that right now you are going to a meeting, and tomorrow morning you have another meeting scheduled. This evening you have arranged to bring your mother to the hospital. Then list alternatives, offering to complete the project at a later date or by another arrangement. In other words, you say that you can attend to his request after the meeting scheduled tomorrow morning, so that you could probably meet his request by four in the afternoon.

Shy People

Shyness is an internal state that leads people to withdraw from or avoid contact with unfamiliar people or circumstances. They obsess about their appearance and behaviour. Some shy people may blush which may increase their shyness further. Shy people freeze up when conversing with strangers in social situations and tend to be self-conscious, self-centred and find it difficult to make eye contact. Shy people are more likely to have low self-esteem than others. Because of this, sometimes they may mistakenly come across as snobbish, haughty and detached. In fact they are just nervous.

Shy people are excessively self-conscious, think negatively and worry obsessively what others think about them. In fact, other people spend most time thinking about themselves rather than thinking about you. Because of this self-consciousness, shy people tend to avoid social events. They want to avoid the limelight and being the focus of attention. Consequently shy people find it difficult to make friends, are thus often lonely and subject to bouts of depression. Reeves (2004) reports that research shows that having at least one close friend is associated with a range of health benefits. These include lower recovery times from cardiac illness, lower incidence of mental illness and a greater resistance to the common cold. So shyness is a health hazard as well as being a major barrier to a successful social life. According to Carducci et al. (1995) nurture rather than nature is the main determinant of shyness, so that you can do something about it.

Overcoming Shyness

To overcome shyness you should:

- Get involved socially. Become genuinely interested in other people. The only way to beat shyness is to go out and talk to other people. You must genuinely want to improve your interpersonal relationship skills and take personal responsibility for doing so. In fact, the best way to make friends is to treat all people you meet as potential friends. You must really want to beat shyness, learn how to do it, try it, and practise it. Behavioural change is difficult and will take time and commitment. Some experts maintain that it takes at least 21 days of continuous practice to change behaviour.

> **"The way you overcome shyness is to become so wrapped up in something that you forget to be afraid." — Lady Bird Johnson**

- Plan your conversations in advance so that you have something to say. Keep up-to-date with current events, think through your opinions and have them ready and mentally rehearsed for the event. Start thinking about others rather than dwelling on your own fears and insecurities. Directing your focus outwards and observing others helps you stop thinking about yourself. Be proactive and learn to take the initiative in social situations. Unless you do something nothing is going to change. Introduce yourself rather than waiting for others to do so, and initiate conversations and you will find that most others are only too willing to do likewise. Initially, just move slightly outside your comfort zone in non-threatening social situations.

- Practise small talk such as remarks about the weather or current events to get the conversation off the ground. Listen, observe and be genuinely interested in the other person. You don't have to do much of the talking as most people just appreciate a friendly ear. Ask questions and elaborate on replies to keep the conversation going. Maintain a reasonable amount of eye contact. However, don't stare as most people find staring uncomfortable. Eye contact shows that you are listening and interested.

- Learn to relax. Use meditation, visualisation and breathing exercises to calm your mind. Even a simple thing like taking a deep breath before entering a social situation will help. Smiling will help you relax and also relax others. Even forcing a smile actually puts you in a better mood. Using humour is often a fast track to being liked.

> **"You can make more friends in two months by becoming interested in other people than you can in two years by trying to get other people interested in you." — Dale Carnegie**

- Learn to handle rejection. Use it as a learning experience. We are not all compatible with each other. Accept that some people may not like you, just as you may not like some people. Some people may have different opinions than yours. In addition people may be in a bad mood or may be just having a bad day. Don't take it personally. Accept that you will meet difficult people from time to time. Move on until you find somebody more inviting to talk to. Remember, the only person you can change is yourself. You have no control over the behaviour, thoughts, attitudes or opinions of others.

- Learn to give and take compliments. Most people love to get genuine compliments. It may be just a remark about a nice hairstyle, or shoes, or piece of clothing. It certainly beats being ignored. As well as giving compliments you should learn how to take them. Acknowledge the compliment with "thank you very much" or "that's very kind of you".

- Think positively. Visualise yourself as a positive outgoing person rather than a shy diffident one. Stop anticipating the worst for social encounters. Nobody is going to bite you when you start a conversation. Visualise positive outcomes rather than negative. Accept that most people are friendly, and have positive intentions towards you. Develop an unconditional positive regard for people. Interrupt negative thoughts by trying to see the funny side of the situation. Somebody once said, "don't take life too seriously, as you'll never get out of it alive".

- Sometimes shy people tend to be perfectionists. Accept that nobody is perfect and you should not demand perfect standards from yourself or others. You don't have to be the perfect conversationalist or tell the perfect joke to engage successfully with somebody. The film industry provides a good model of what we should do with mistakes: cut, do a retake, and then laugh at your failures. The only real mistake is where we fail to learn.

- Control your emotions. Stay cool, calm and collected when other people try to provoke you. Think positive thoughts. Self-control means you stay in command and don't upset yourself or other people. Learn to control your anger, fear, anxiety and self-consciousness. Accept that negative results sometimes happen. Stay calm, move on and focus on the next opportunity.

- Relate to people at an emotional level. Empathise with others and respect their feelings. Some people are left-brained and think in a logical way. Such people find it almost impossible to overlook a factual inaccuracy during a conversation. However, most people are governed by their emotions and like others to make them feel good about themselves. This means that it makes sense not to be continually looking for sources of disagreement even if you are correct. This doesn't mean that you compromise your integrity. It just means that you should know when it is not appropriate or worthwhile to take a stand. It is more important to make people feel positive and good about themselves by creating and maintaining good relationships than proving your point. Most people crave acceptance and respect.

Summary

Popular people know how to relate effectively with others. They treat others as they would like others to treat them. They realise if they help others to meet their needs they are more likely to be helped in return.

To communicate effectively with others we must talk to them in a sincere and friendly way. Conversation is about exchanging information, thoughts, concerns, feelings, ideas, courtesies, pleasantries and compliments. SIMPLE is an acronym that may be used to help you create a good impression on others. This stands for speech, involve your listener, mirror body language, positive handshake, lean forward and eye contact.

Assertiveness is about expressing your needs, preferences, wishes and feelings in a way that is neither threatening, offensive nor harmful to others. You should be conversant with the Bill of Rights meaning, among other things, that you are aware that your needs are just as important as anybody else's.

Shy people freeze up when conversing with strangers and tend to be self-conscious and self-centred. They think negatively and worry obsessively what others think about them. To become more outgoing you should take the initiative in starting conversations with strangers.

FIVE STEPS TO IMPROVING INTERPERSONAL RELATIONSHIPS

1. The next time you engage in a conversation let the other person do most of the talking and study the reaction that you get.

2. Seek out feedback from your friends about the strengths and weaknesses of your interpersonal relationship skills. Reflect on any negative feedback received and try to improve for the future.

3. Practise smiling. A smile is probably the easiest thing you can do to encourage positive relationships.

4. List three things you need to do to create a good impression. Actively incorporate these into your daily behaviours.

5. Before your next social engagement plan topics of conversation in advance to make sure you have something interesting to say.

Case Study: Overcoming Shyness

Cathy worked as an administrator in a large company. She had been with the company five years and was concerned about her lack of progress in her career. She was quiet spoken, diffident, had a retiring and shy disposition and always puts the needs of others before her own. She didn't believe in talking about her accom-

plishments and found it hard to accept compliments. Nevertheless she was on very good terms with her work colleagues and was popular and held in high regard by all she came into contact with.

Four times over the past five years she had been passed over for promotion even though she felt that she was as well qualified as the people who got the promotional positions. She made an appointment with the Human Resource Manager (HRM) to find out why she was not getting promoted. While her present job was interesting, she felt that she was well capable of doing jobs at a higher level.

At the interview with the HRM, Cathy made her feelings and concerns known. The HRM listened politely before addressing her concerns. He agreed with her that she was as well qualified as the people who got the promotions but made the point that she failed to come across well at interviews. She came across during the interview process as being shy, withdrawn, indecisive and lacking confidence. She usually spoke in a very quiet voice so that the interviewers had difficulty hearing what she had to say. This wasn't helped by the fact that she stared at the table during most of the interview rather than maintain eye contact with the interviewers. He suggested that she should undertake some assertiveness training to improve her confidence and communication skills. If Cathy was willing to undertake such training he said that the company would willingly pay for it. He said on the positive side there were no concerns about her work performance and she got along well with her immediate work colleagues. In the meantime he was prepared to coach her in interview technique. Cathy was glad to accept.

Cathy agreed to attend the assertiveness course, which was run by an outside training company who specialised in this type of training. There were ten participants on the course including herself. The course was run over four days with plenty of role-play and opportunities to practise and reflect on the skills taught. The course opened Cathy's eyes to her communication shortfalls and lack of assertiveness skills and more importantly to the actions she should put into practice to remedy the situation. She now realised that she should learn how to fight her own corner and assertively argue her case as appropriate without causing offence to others.

Over the following months Cathy practised her new assertive-ness skills and was very happy with the results. Her peers noticed that Cathy had become a more confident, decisive and assertive person. She now spoke with conviction and accepted that her needs were just as important as others. In her personal life her friends and colleagues also noticed a new assertive and confident Cathy. Within a year she applied and was successful in getting the next promotion. This time she got excellent feedback on her in-terview performance. She is now looking forward to a fruitful and rewarding career in the company.

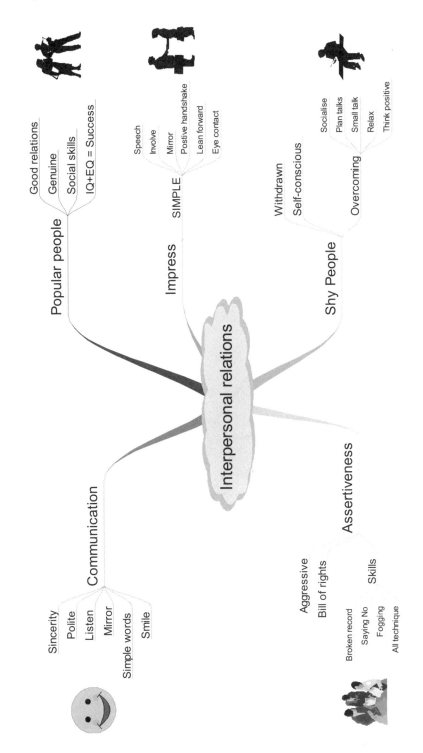

Interpersonal relations

Popular people
- Good relations
- Genuine
- Social skills
- IQ+EQ = Success

Impress — SIMPLE
- Speech
- Involve
- Mirror
- Positive handshake
- Lean forward
- Eye contact

Shy People
- Withdrawn
- Self-conscious
- Overcoming
  - Socialise
  - Plan talks
  - Small talk
  - Relax
  - Think positive

Communication
- Sincerity
- Polite
- Listen
- Mirror
- Simple words
- Smile

Assertiveness
- Aggressive
- Bill of rights
- Skills
  - Broken record
  - Saying No
  - Fogging
  - All technique

7

SELF-ESTEEM

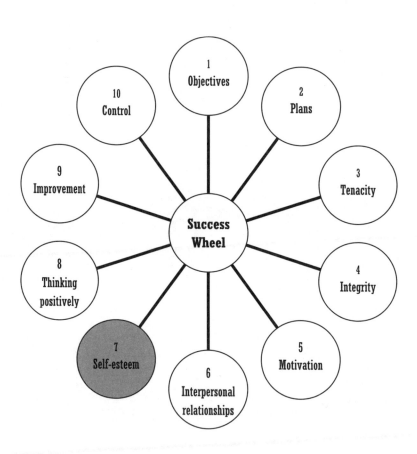

♦ What are the characteristics of high self-esteem?

♦ What are the characteristics of low self-esteem?

♦ What is self-efficacy?

♦ Why are feelings of self-worth important?

♦ How can I improve my self-esteem?

"You must believe in yourself, my son, or no one will believe in you. Be self-confident, self-reliant, and even if you don't make it, you will know you have done your best. Now, go to it." — Mary Hardy MacArthur

---

S stands for self-esteem and is the seventh letter of our acronym OPTIMISTIC. Personal development experts believe that self-esteem is an important ingredient of a rewarding and successful life. It may even be more important than intelligence or talent. Self-esteem is the value we place on ourselves. We can have high self-esteem in some areas of our lives and low self-esteem in others. People with low self-esteem are riddled with self-doubt and negative beliefs. Self-efficacy is a belief in your own capabilities. If you believe you can accomplish something you are more likely to get a positive outcome. There are certain actions you can take to improve your self-esteem.

High Self-Esteem

Self-esteem is the value we place on specific aspects of ourselves. In the eyes of others you are only worth as much as your self-esteem. There is a relationship between our self-esteem and our self-image (the way we see ourselves). A positive self-image is an essential ingredient of high self-esteem. Our self-image is moulded by past experiences, successes, failures and how other people react to us. Feeling guilty about past wrongs that you may have done to others may negatively affect your self-image. Most of us have skeletons in our closets. Rather than ruminating on these we should acknowledge our feelings and move on. Take corrective action to make amends for the wrong if possible. In any event forgive yourself and consider all the good things you have done in your life. See yourself in a compassionate and understanding light. You are not your mistakes. Strengthen your commitment to meaningful goals in the future. Self-image is not permanent. It will change in line with our life experiences. We always act like the person we conceive ourselves to be. A poor self-image will act as a barrier to peak performance.

> **"Self-esteem is the reputation we acquire with ourselves."**
> **— Nathaniel Branden**

Our self-image defines and limits our possibilities. Improve your self-image and expand your range of possibilities. If we see ourselves as a failure we will act out that script. On the other hand, if we see ourselves as a success we will likewise act out that script. In other words, you can programme your self-image for success or failure. The choice is yours. Thoughts and feelings affect behaviour. Our self-image determines our level of confidence. We create the life for good or bad that supports our self-image. A good self-image releases the talents and energies we already possess. If we see ourselves favourably then we are likely to have high self-esteem. Focus on your successes rather than your failures.

Psychologist Abraham Maslow included self-esteem as a key element in his hierarchy of needs. In Maslow's view self-esteem includes self-respect, trust, relevance and worth; all of which are necessary for a meaningful, purposeful and fulfilling life. Thus building self-esteem is one of the most important aspects of the human growth process. It has been said that self-esteem is to the mind what food is to the body. Moreover, self-actualisation can only begin when some degree of self-esteem has been achieved.

In our head we create our own possibilities and limitations. On the down side people often develop phobias such as a fear of spiders, fear of flying, fear of heights or fear of confined spaces (claustrophobia) in their heads. This demonstrates the mind-body connection as these reactions are produced by people's thoughts and not by physical causes. This means that your beliefs can strongly affect outcomes. Nevertheless, you can reinforce true self-esteem by authentic achievement and genuine praise. Therefore, praising people for mediocre or trivial accomplishments may be counterproductive. The essence of self-esteem comes from a feeling that you've done your personal best and that you deserve any praise or credit received.

"There is overwhelming evidence that the higher the level of self-esteem, the more likely one will be to treat others with respect, kindness, and generosity." — Nathaniel Branden

---

A realistic assessment of abilities should form the foundation of self-esteem. People with high self-esteem take responsibility for their actions, don't indulge in blaming others for their problems and make their own decisions. They feel they deserve any success that they have. People with high self-esteem are more willing to speak up in groups and criticise and propose solutions for action. They are more concerned with what they think about themselves rather than what other people think about them.

Self-esteem is not static throughout our lives but may rise and fall as we go through different life stages. The teenage years are often a time of low self-esteem when teenagers are trying to establish themselves in life and assert their identity. At the other end of the scale, when people retire they often miss the challenge, security and routine of work and may develop feelings of low self-esteem because they feel that they are no longer making a valuable contribution to the world.

Baumeister et al. (2003) found that the link between self-esteem and happiness is strong. People with high self-esteem are substantially happier than other people. They are also less likely to be depressed in response to stressful, traumatic events.

Exercise and Self-esteem

Jourdan (2005) reports that there is increasing evidence to show that getting close to nature can make us feel less stressed and better about ourselves. A University of Essex study shows that "green" exercise can boost mood, physical fitness and self-esteem. Professor Jules Pretty, who led the research team, measured the mood and self-esteem of 263 people who took part on 10 different "green" activities, such as walking, mountain-biking and canal boating. They found that there was a significant improvement in self-esteem in 9 out of 10 cases. The majority of people found that anxiety levels dropped and they felt less depressed and more upbeat.

Interestingly, angling is one of the best ways to enjoy the feel-good factor of the natural world. The sport, which boasts an impressive following of 3.8 million people in Britain, tops the study's list for boosting self-esteem and mood. It has long been thought that fishing is a type of therapy and a great way to reduce stress. Essex University's research also found that, when measuring the impact of green activities on mental well-being, their duration was not significant. They found that a half-hour walk gave the same benefit as a six-hour fishing trip and that even gazing at the countryside is good for your health.

Tests conducted by the research team on 100 health volunteers who ran on treadmills showed that looking at a pleasant rural view caused blood pressure to fall. On the other hand, looking at an unpleasant urban environment caused blood pressure to rise by an average of eight points. This means that a view from a window, or even a static image, makes a difference to your well-being. The findings are supported by a study at Johns Hopkins University in the USA. Doctors focused on two groups of patients who were in hospital, awaiting operations. The first group was shown an image of a beautiful landscape, while they listened to piped sounds of birds and running water. The second group, however, was left in a room with no view and no sound. Following their operations, the first group required significantly less pain control and left hospital sooner than the second group.

We are all aware of the ancient maxim *mens sana in corpore sano* (a healthy mind in a healthy body). It is now accepted that exercise does indeed play a positive role in maintaining high self-esteem. Regular exercise improves cardiovascular condition, reduces stress, anxiety and depression and improves digestion and sleep. Exercise also improves the blood flow to the brain improving alertness, concentration and memory performance. Our modern lifestyles that are so dependent on the car do not lend themselves to regular exercise. Exercise should become routine and a natural part of your lifestyle. Even moderate aerobic exercise, including regular long brisk walks and frequently climbing stairs will keep you reasonably fit.

Self-talk

Confidence is a state of mind and so people with high self-esteem flood their minds with positive thoughts such as "I like myself", "I'm capable and competent", and "I've something special to offer the world". Self-talk has a way of becoming a self-fulfilling prophecy so it is important to monitor your inner voice as negative thinking can undermine your self-esteem if left unchallenged. As Gandhi said, "The history of the world is full of men who rose to leadership, by sheer force of self-confidence, bravery and tenacity."

Self-talk and affirmations will help you retain your sense of worth. Combine affirmations with creative mental imagery for best results. Affirmations should be personal, positive and said in the present tense. The subconscious mind cannot process a negative instruction. So make sure you are telling your subconscious mind what to do, think and be rather than telling it what not to do, think and be. High self-esteem is not the same as boasting, bragging or arrogance. In fact, these are often signs of low self-esteem. Channing Pollack said, "Calm self-confidence is as far from conceit as the desire to earn a decent living is remote from greed."

Personal Development and Self-esteem

Personal development experts all concur that self-esteem is an important ingredient to a successful and rewarding life. People with high self-esteem are willing to respond to challenges and seek out opportunities for improvement, learning and development. They believe they are capable of successfully acquiring new skills, knowledge or expertise. They see learning and development opportunities as a challenge to be embraced.

People with high self-esteem are more likely to be sociable and co-operative. They are more expressive, good at interpersonal relationships and always look for the good in others. They realise that good relationships are central to good health and high self-esteem. They accept compliments gracefully and are not reluctant to praise and compliment themselves when nobody else is prepared to do so.

> **"Persons of high self-esteem are not driven to make themselves superior to others. . . . Their joy is being who they are, not in being better than someone else." — Nathaniel Branden**

People with high self-esteem compete in their minds with themselves. They are not envious of the abilities, achievements or success of others.

Self-worth

People of high self-esteem have a good sense of self-worth. In line with the American dream people with self-worth believe they have a right to life, liberty and the pursuit of happiness. They feel good about themselves, are satisfied with their own lives and know their own value. They compare themselves favourably with others. They believe they are deserving of happiness and achievement, worthy of love and the friendship of others. They are less self-evaluative and more self-actualised; that is, they believe in developing their own unique talents.

They realise they are unique human beings and are proud of their attributes and achievements. This self-acceptance means they like themselves because of who they are but at the same time accept their limitations. They enjoy and take pride in their achievements but at the same time know that they can't be good at everything. They are more self-confident and persistent and thus achieve more. They are not unduly concerned with what others think of them. However, we are gregarious beings and whether we admit it or not we are influenced to a lesser or greater extent by what other people think of us. Positive feedback from others does contribute to our feelings of self-worth.

Self-efficacy

Self-efficacy is an important aspect of self-esteem. This is our belief about whether or not we can perform a particular task, bring about a successful outcome and generally cope with life's challenges. On the other hand, self-doubt hinders the successful completion of tasks and creates fear of failure instead of confidence of success.

Our level of self-efficacy will determine our aspirations in life. People with high self-efficacy have ambitious goals, implement action plans to achieve them and visualise successful outcomes. They observe and learn from role models that have accomplished similar goals. The biography of great people is the best source of both information and inspiration on role models. They often display high resilience in the face of difficulties with the ability to bounce back from setbacks. Choose as your role models people who have achieved something that may be difficult but relevant and feasible for you to do. Comparing yourself with people with very exceptional talents may be counterproductive and undermining.

"To be ambitious for wealth, and yet always expecting to be poor, to be always doubting your ability to get what you long for, is like trying to reach east by travelling west. There is no philosophy, which will help man to succeed when he always doubts his ability to do so, and thus attracting failure." — Charles Baudouin

---

The more competent you are the higher your sense of self-efficacy. You expect success rather than failure. Research has even found that over-confidence is sometimes desirable as it makes us try harder which in turn improves our chances of success. People with self-efficacy believe that success is due to the exercise of their own skills, knowledge and competencies and not due to outside factors. They believe they can shape their own destinies and make things happen. They identify areas in which they can excel. If they lack particular skills they go about acquiring them. They believe that competence is incremental and can be increased through experience. They believe in their capacity to understand, learn and make decisions.

Context Specific

Self-efficacy leads to a sense of control over one's life. Self-efficacy is brought about by four factors, namely previous success in a similar situation, learning from the success of others, strong expectation and positive emotional feelings. Depending on their area of expertise people can have high feelings of self-efficacy in one situation and feelings of low self-efficacy in another. For example, a marketing executive is more likely to have feelings of high self-efficacy when confronted with marketing issues. When confronted with financial issues he may experience feelings of low self-efficacy and lack of confidence in line with his lack of knowledge and expertise of the area.

Similarly, a professional speaker may be confident when giving a speech at a business seminar but may be plagued with self-doubts about his inability to give up smoking. A mathematician is likely to have a greater sense of self-efficacy in maths rather than in repairing cars.

Believe and You Shall Achieve

If we believe we can succeed then we are more likely to do so. People with self-efficacy will have strong confidence in their abilities to perform and will manage potentially difficult situations in a calm and purposeful manner. On the other hand, people who lack confidence will approach such situations with fear and apprehension, thereby reducing the probability that they will be successful. If we think we won't succeed then we are unlikely to even attempt it in the first instance. Achievement is the best way to promote self-efficacy as success breeds success. Thus self-efficacy will determine our willingness to attempt challenging tasks, our commitment and persistence during the attempt and our ability to recover quickly from failure and learn from our mistakes. On the other hand, repeated failure does nothing for our self-confidence and will lower our sense of self-efficacy further. However, if you are used to being successful the occasional failure has little impact on your sense of self-efficacy.

Learned Helplessness

Learned helplessness is the opposite of self-efficacy. It is thought to be a major factor in depression. Here some people have learned that anything they do makes no difference and they become passive and give up and sometimes don't even try. They fail to exert control because of previous failures and excessive self-doubt, thus reinforcing the belief that they will fail again. McLeod (1986) found that experiments in learned helplessness produced diverse effects in humans. In response to repeated failure, some people gave up, others kept trying and still others intensified their efforts to succeed.

Limits of Self-esteem

Most authorities would agree that self-esteem in a necessary condition for a happy and fulfilling life. But it's not a panacea. Even people with high self-esteem are not immune to the trials and tribulations of daily living. They too will experience anxiety, depression or fear when overwhelmed by issues that they don't know how to cope with. They too may need the support of others to survive and cope with such life episodes.

Self-esteem is perception rather than reality. It refers to a person's belief, which may or may not be true. For example, a person may belief that they are intelligent and attractive without this being necessarily true. People's beliefs shape their actions in many important ways for good or for bad. Baumeister et al. (2003) found that people high in self-esteem regard themselves as better liked and more popular than others, but most of these advantages exist mainly in their own minds, and objective data generally fail to confirm them. In some cases, people with high self-esteem are actually disliked more than others.

People with high self-esteem may find it more difficult to deal with setbacks. Coover et al. (2000) found that self-esteem alone does not predict success. In fact, those with particularly high self-esteem are 26 per cent more susceptible to the consequences of failure. It seems that negative outcomes can have a devastating effect on their self-image.

Narcissism

Narcissus is an extreme form of self-esteem. Narcissus was a figure in Greek mythology who spent his days pining after his own reflection in a pool, neglected everyone else in his life, preoccupied as he was with himself. Narcissistic people have a very high opinion of themselves. The are self-centred with feelings of self-importance, arrogance, grandiosity, egotism and conceit. Because of their inflated view of themselves they tend to antagonise and alienate others. They are prone to bully others and to retaliate aggressively at the least provocation. They make poor romantic lovers, as they cannot love anybody but themselves. Although demonstrating signs of very high self-esteem, some experts think that narcissistic people actually are people with low self-esteem.

Dark Side of High Self-esteem

There is a dark side to high self-esteem. It seems that too much self-esteem may be damaging to health — especially other people's health. Some experts maintain that such people are in fact self-centred, narcissistic and egotistic with strong feelings of grandiosity rather than having a sense of high self-esteem. Most authorities agree that those who exhibit such characteristics are merely compensating for low self-esteem.

> "Self-esteem is different than conceit. Conceit is the weirdest disease in the world. It makes everyone sick except the one who has it." — Hartman Rector Jr

At the Nuremberg trials the SS officers, such as Rudolf Hess, tried for war crimes after World War II displayed an inflated sense of self-esteem. There is no doubt that Hitler had very high self-esteem but used it in a very destructive way. He built up a following by telling the German people that they were the so-called Master Race, an idea that undoubtedly had a broad and seductive appeal. Other historical tyrants like Stalin and Idi Amin, who bestowed himself with all sorts of military honours including the Victoria Cross, had super-inflated self-esteems.

Dylan Klebold and Eric Harris shot dead 12 students and a teacher at Columbine High School outside Denver in the US in the spring of 1999. Contrary to popular belief, Colvin (2000) reports that neither Harris nor Klebold suffered from a shortage of self-esteem. Indeed, Harris's diaries revealed a person with a hyper-inflated view of himself. Conventional wisdom maintains that a strong sense of self-esteem is supposed to serve as a vaccine against such violent crimes. Self-esteem theorists usually maintain that people who feel good about themselves would be less likely to commit such crimes. We now know that that is not always the case.

Conventional Wisdom and Self-esteem

Toynbee (2001) reports that Professor Emler in his report "Self-Esteem" turns conventional wisdom about self-esteem on its head. Low self-esteem is certainly not the root of all evil. Emler found that there is no evidence that low self-esteem causes anti-social behaviour. Quite the reverse is true. Those who think highly of themselves are the ones most prone to violence and most likely to take risks, believing themselves invulnerable. They are more likely to commit crimes, drive dangerously, and risk their health with drugs and alcohol. Exceptionally low self-esteem is indeed damaging — but only to the victim, not to anybody else. Those with low self-esteem are more likely to commit suicide, to be depressed, to become victims of bullying, domestic violence, loneliness and social ostracism.

Burke (2001) reports that research shows that young people with high self-esteem are more likely to take illicit drugs than those whose self-confidence is low. The findings contradict the conventional wisdom that drug taking is most prevalent among anxious or insecure youth looking for an escape from poor home conditions or a way to feel better about themselves. The survey of 15,000 children aged 14 and 15 conducted by Exeter's Schools Health Education Unit in the UK showed that up to 27 per cent of young people with high self-esteem had used illicit substances compared with only 20 per cent of their less self-confident peers. Two factors are thought to explain the results. More confident children are more likely to be sociable, have more money and thus have more opportunity to experiment with drugs. And they are also more willing to indulge in risk-taking activities, ranging from extreme sports to class A drugs. Research also shows that young committed smokers have high self-esteem.

Emler looked at the relation between self-esteem and academic success. Most surprisingly he concluded that academic success or failure had very little impact on pupil's self-esteem. High self-esteem pupils will explain away failure to suit their previous high opinions of themselves: they make excuses that they were unlucky, suffered some bias or that they didn't try. Odder still, those with low self-esteem were not buoyed up by academic success either. Sadly, they regard it as a fluke and continue with their previous low estimation of their abilities. He concludes that it is exceedingly difficult to shift people's pre-existing view of themselves, even with tangible success. Nor is self-esteem any predictor of how well or badly someone will do academically.

The conventional wisdom that "more is better" as regards self-esteem can be disputed. There are even times when it may be better to deflate bloated egos. Groskop (2004) makes the point that some people have unrealistically high self-esteem. This is demonstrated by the thousands of hopefuls who appear on Simon Cowell's *Pop Idol* talent contest shown on TV each Saturday night. The majority of contestants have no talent but nevertheless have an inflated view of their star potential. When they are rejected by the panel they are distraught and most of them think there has been a genuine mistake and can't understand why the panel hasn't recognised their unique talent and charisma. They cling stubbornly to their unrealistic dream and their flawed estimation of themselves. They think that acting like a winner will make you one. Maybe they would be happier if they loved themselves a bit less and took a more realistic view of their mundane talents.

Nature versus Nurture

Emler concludes that genetic predisposition has the single strongest effect on self-esteem. Next are parental attitudes. If parents love, reinforce, praise and respect a young child, the effect lasts for life. Physical and above all sexual abuse of children is devastatingly and permanently damaging to a child's self-esteem.

Men have slightly more self-esteem than women. Low self-esteem in women does increase the risk of teenage pregnancy, while low self-esteem in boys increases the risk of unemployment later in life. Anxiety about appearance undermines women's self-esteem. A curious finding is that there is little correlation between how people think they look and how they actually look. Our level of self-esteem determines our perceptions about appearance. Emler found that people have profoundly unrealistic views of how others see them, both negative and positive. How we think we are perceived is shaped by self-esteem.

Doheny (2004) reports that Roy F. Baumeister of Florida State University found that high self-esteem probably does make you happier and may lead to a healthier lifestyle but it won't necessarily improve your career or interpersonal relationships. Baumeister found that the trend towards expecting praise before earning it is not good. He maintains that concentrating on self-control and performance rather than self-esteem will do more for you in the long term.

> **"Self-esteem is as important to our well-being as legs are to a table. It is essential for physical and mental health and for happiness." — Louise Hart**

Science News (2003) reports that Baumeister found that high self-esteem — whether present in individuals from the start or induced through educational programmes — generally doesn't lead to improved school or job performance. However, academic and job successes often boost self-esteem. People who evaluate themselves extremely positively aren't more likely than others to have satisfying relationships, assume leadership positions or avoid bouts of depression. Overall, high self-esteem enhances pleasant feelings and generally increases a person's willingness to initiate either positive *or negative* behaviour. For instance, schoolyard bullies, as well as those who stand up to them, frequently report high self-esteem.

Low Self-esteem

People with low self-esteem resist change, avoid challenge and are generally risk-averse. They are reluctant to accept praise, compliments and positive feedback, speak up in groups, and don't acknowledge or take pride in their own achievements. At the same time they hunger for love and approval that they sometimes fail to find and seek out status symbols as a compensation to fill the void. They usually lack the confidence to undertake learning and development experiences. As a consequence they never reach their true potential and often spend their lives in low-level frustrating jobs.

People with low self-esteem blame and complain a lot while at the same time doing nothing constructive to change their lives. Thus others find it difficult to put up with them and avoid their company. They often view themselves as victims — of their upbringing or circumstances — which makes it harder for them to take control of their life and change.

People with low self-esteem often fear authority figures and are uncomfortable and feel inferior in their presence. They often suffer from feelings of self-doubt, insecurity, helplessness, fear, failure, frustration and rejection. Consequently, they are often poor socialisers. They tend to be more realistic about their shortcomings than people with high self-esteem but this is probably a drawback, if anything, as it limits their aspirations. People with low self-esteem tend to lack initiative and are thus often more dependent on others.

People with low self-esteem are more likely to suffer loneliness and depression and to take their own life. They are often shy with doubts about their ability to make meaningful relationships. They are less likely to be creative, make effective decisions and have satisfactory interpersonal relationships. They are more prone to excessive drinking, promiscuous sex, eating disorders such as anorexia nervosa and bulimia, drug abuse, teenage pregnancy, bullying and domestic violence. They are more likely to comfort eat to fill the emotional void in their lives and to counteract feelings of anger, stress, depression, sadness, loneliness, boredom and emptiness.

Self-sabotage

People with low or damaged self-esteem often self-sabotage. They have a self-image of someone who doesn't deserve success. They don't believe they are worthy to be successful and consequently often indulge in self-destructive behaviour and throw it all away. They have negative thoughts about themselves. They never finish what they start. Seemingly successful people such as film stars, models and rock stars often self-

destruct on drugs, alcohol, addiction, self-abuse and other excesses. Sometimes self-sabotage is not something you do consciously, but your subconscious takes over to confirm your
negative self-image of a person who doesn't succeed. People
can become very comfortable with not succeeding. It confirms
the view they have of themselves that success is for somebody
else.

"Low self-esteem is like driving through life with your hand-break on." — Maxwell Maltz

---

People with low self-esteem may self-handicap to protect
their image and to save face. Kimble et al. (1998) found that recent psychological research has shown that many adults self-
handicap. When faced with an evaluative threat, people may
self-handicap by creating a disadvantage for themselves before
the evaluation rather than preparing to do their best. The use of
alcohol or drugs is an example of such self-handicapping behaviour, as is inadequate preparation for an important task such
as a student failing to prepare for an examination.

"Musturbation"

People with low self-esteem often set themselves impossible
standards and make negative comparisons with role models.
They are likely to use words like, "Never", "I have to", "I ought
to", "I must" and "I should". In psychology, this has become
known as "musturbation". Examples include, "I must be liked
by everybody that I meet", "I must always be neat and tidy",
and "I must be perfect at everything". The rigid thinking involved in musturbation is not conducive to a successful and
happy life and can often be traced back to early parental influences. The goals are unrealistic and the attitudes are those of a
person trying to please others or a victim rather than a person
with free choice. Choose words like, "I choose", "I decide", "I
want", "I like" and "I prefer". These words put you in the driving seat and very much in control.

How to Raise Your Self-esteem

- Do a strengths and weaknesses analysis on your self-esteem. Identify the areas of your life where your self-esteem needs building. Focus on your strengths as you go about addressing your weaknesses.

"No one can make you feel inferior without your permission." — **Eleanor Roosevelt**

- Beliefs lead to thoughts, thoughts lead to feelings and feelings lead to behaviour. Change your beliefs and you will change your behaviour. Consider the beliefs you have in relation to your self-image, job, relationships, social status and possessions. For example, "I'm no good at maths", "I'm too old to start again", or "I'm too shy to relate successfully to others". Change these to more positive ones as appropriate. Even though beliefs are hardwired into our brains from an early age by parents and influential others they can be challenged and changed for the better.

- Accept graciously the praise, compliments and positive feedback you get from others. Just say "Thank you very much". These may prove to be rare occasions in life, so accept and relish them while you have the chance. Praise yourself occasionally when nobody else does so.

- Accept that there is no such thing as failure, only feedback. Reflect and learn from your experiences.

- Have a library of past successful experiences to go through in your mind. Visualise and play these in your mind when you feel you need a morale boost. Unfortunately, the vast majority of people fail to employ this strategy to psych themselves up.

- Imagine future successes. The subconscious mind can't tell the difference between a real and an imagined event. Imagination is greater than knowledge. Creative imagination is the driving force behind all change. You can change your image by replaying past successes and visualising future successes. Your behaviour and self-image is controlled by your mind.

"To establish true self-esteem we must concentrate on our successes and forget about the failures and the negatives in our lives." — Denis Waitley

---

- Act "as if" you have a high sense of self-esteem in situations where you want to. Walk tall, hold your head up, smile and speak with conviction and without hesitation.

- Study and model the behaviour of high self-esteem people. Observe their mannerisms, body language, speech, style and general demeanour.

- Set realistic objectives and break them down into manageable parts. Don't try to achieve too much too quickly. Rome wasn't built in a day. So you need also to be patient but persistent. Small successes breed further success. Be prepared to take risks. There are no rewards without risks.

- Use positive affirmations and self-talk to feed your mind with positive thoughts.

- Accept that you will meet people from time to time that do not like you, are rude to you or insensitive. In this life you need to develop a thick skin. In this regard, politicians should act as your role models. Move on to people who appreciate your company. It is impossible to change other people; they can only change themselves.

- Reframe negative situations in a positive way. See obstacles as challenges and mistakes as learning opportunities. For example, a delayed flight might be reframed as an opportunity to catch up on some reading.

- Avoid musturbation. Adopt the attitude that there are few "have tos" in life. Ultimately there is only one "have to" and that is to die. In the meantime you should make the best of life and live on the basis of "choose to" and "want to".

- Realise if things are going to happen you must make them happen. So do something. Take full responsibility for your life and your aspirations while using the support of others when it is available. Don't let other people's expectations determine the direction of your life. Make your own decisions in life.

- Join groups that promote positive self-esteem. Avoid people with negative attitudes.

Summary

Self-esteem is the value we place on specific aspects of ourselves. Depending on their area of expertise people can have high feelings of self-esteem in one situation and feelings of low self-esteem in another. Our self-image impacts on our self-esteem. If we see ourselves favourably then we are likely to have confidence and high self-esteem. Personal development experts all agree that self-esteem is an important ingredient to a successful and rewarding life.

People of high self-esteem have a good sense of self-worth. They feel good about themselves, are satisfied with their own lives and know their own value. Self-efficacy is an important aspect of self-esteem. This is an inherent belief in our own capabilities. If we believe we can succeed then we are more likely to do so. It is impossible to succeed if you do not believe in yourself.

> **"We often become what we believe ourselves to be. If I believe I cannot do something, it makes me incapable of doing it. When I believe I can, I acquire the ability to do it even if I didn't have it in the beginning." — Mahatma Gandhi**

People with low self-esteem resist change, avoid challenge and are generally risk-averse. They are reluctant to accept praise, compliments and positive feedback, and don't acknowledge or take pride in their own achievements. People with low self-esteem blame others and complain a lot while at the same time doing nothing constructive to change their lives. Don't just sit there and complain, do something about it!

There are many ways to raise your self-esteem including nurturing positive thoughts, taking responsibility for your actions and practising affirmations and visualisations.

FIVE STEPS TO IMPROVING YOUR SELF-ESTEEM

1. **Think back over your past successes and create a success library in your head. Visualise and replay these in your mind when you feel you need a morale boost or to counteract negative thoughts.**

2. **Draw up a weekly schedule of physical exercise that you will do. Exercise will improve your health and mood and make you feel good about yourself.**

3. **Mix with positive people to maintain and enhance your self-esteem.**

4. **Build up your expertise in your favourite subject. Becoming an expert in a topic will do wonders for your self-esteem.**

5. **Compete with yourself rather than with others. Continually improve on your previous best performance.**

Case Study: A Sense of Insecurity

Tom was always ambitious and when he left college with a first class degree in business studies he was determined to get to the top. His first job was as a trainee manager in a large supermarket in a provincial town that was part of a national chain of stores. He devoted himself to the job, worked long hours and within three years was made a manager of one of the stores. He now felt he would need to do a master's degree if he wanted to go further in the company. He enrolled in the local college and began doing a part-time MBA degree. This took two years and he found the going quite challenging. Between work and study he really had no time for any personal life. His whole being was consumed by his ambition to get ahead.

On completion of his studies he was offered a job as marketing director in the company's head office which was based in the capital city. Tom willingly took the job and saw it as another step in his ambition of becoming the chief executive of the company. Tom seldom took vacations but preferred to work instead. Tom had a fear of being unsuccessful and was driven by the memory of his father who lost his job and struggled to fill his days. His mother was forced to go out and do menial work and the money earned was barely enough to survive on. Tom was determined that this would never happen to him. Tom's devotion to the job didn't go unnoticed and within another five years he was appointed assistant chief executive. The chief executive was 63 and would retire within two years. Tom was obviously being groomed for the top job.

In the meantime Tom had married his private secretary, five years younger than him, and was now the proud father of two sons. His wife left the company to become a full-time mother and housewife. This suited Tom as he now had the comfort of a stable home life and a loving wife. Tom's preoccupation with his career was now complete and he spent more and more hours at work. In fact some nights he stayed overnight in a hotel just across the road from the company's HQ. He had an understanding wife who knew the culture of the company and who supported Tom in his ambitions to become chief executive. As expected on the retirement of the current chief executive, Tom got the job.

Tom's wife thought he would now slow down since he had achieved the ambition of his life. However, over the following years Tom's behaviour got more compulsive and he became the classic workaholic. His self-image and self-worth were totally identified with his job. He had no outside interests or hobbies. However, the job was not meeting his psychological needs. Money, power and prestige are no substitute for feeling that there is meaning in your life. He felt increasingly insecure, isolated and stressed and feared the up and coming executives were after his job. Tom was often feeling drained and got little satisfaction from his work.

Eventually one night at the office the inevitable happened and he collapsed and was taken to hospital with a suspected heart attack. The doctor advised him that he would have to change his diet and lifestyle if he wanted to live, as the stress of his job would kill him. Tom's crisis proved to be a critical moment in his life and he realised that his priorities were all wrong. Success should not be about acquiring wealth and status but should be about living a fulfilling and happy life. Tom was just 46 years of age and didn't want to die and leave a wife and family behind. He realised that he had been given a second chance at life.

During the time in hospital Tom had plenty of time to reflect on the doctor's advice and on his life in general. He realised that his ambition had been driven by the negative emotions of a childhood fear of poverty and of being unsuccessful. Contrary to his expectations, landing the top job didn't meet his real needs, didn't make him satisfied, and didn't automatically bestow a healthy sense of self-worth and happiness. Self-worth comes from within rather than from trappings of status and wealth.

In his personal life his wife and children had become alienated through years of neglect and inattention. He discovered that time is the greatest gift you can bestow. On reflection, he was surprised that his wife hadn't left him years ago and that his children were still on talking terms with him. He now appreciated that his wife and family were the most precious things in his life.

Despite the duration of his illness the company continued to survive and prosper without his guiding presence and this fact reinforced Tom's new perspective on life. When he was discharged from hospital he was determined to change his lifestyle, enjoy his wealth, foster friendships and make up for lost time with his family. Life is for living and Tom was determined to live it to the full while he still had the opportunity. Tom is now back at work and works a normal week, devoting the weekends to his wife and family. He has acquired outside interests and made new friends and is now living a more balanced and satisfying life.

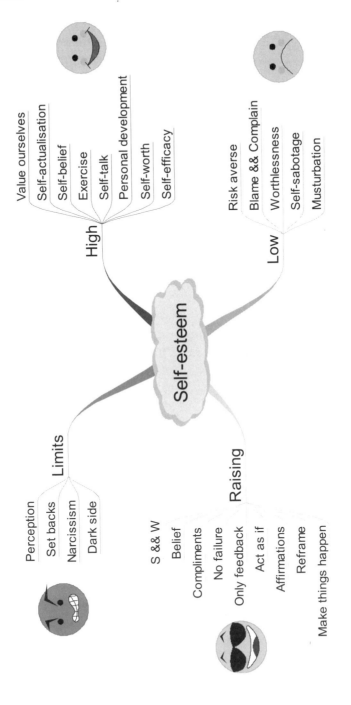

Self-esteem

High
- Value ourselves
- Self-actualisation
- Self-belief
- Exercise
- Self-talk
- Personal development
- Self-worth
- Self-efficacy

Low
- Risk averse
- Blame && Complain
- Worthlessness
- Self-sabotage
- Musturbation

Limits
- Perception
- Set backs
- Narcissism
- Dark side

Raising
- S && W
- Belief
- Compliments
- No failure
- Only feedback
- Act as if
- Affirmations
- Reframe
- Make things happen

8

THINKING POSITIVELY

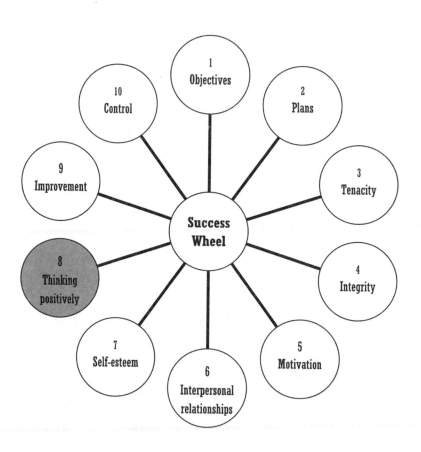

♦ What is positive thinking?

♦ How do optimists and pessimists think?

♦ What is the ABCDE technique?

♦ How can I become happy?

♦ What are the poor thinking habits?

"The pessimist sees difficulty in every opportunity. The optimist sees opportunity in every difficulty." — Winston Churchill

---

T stands for thinking positively and is the eighth letter of our acronym OPTIMISTIC. Self-esteem and positive thinking are intrinsically connected. Self-esteem is the value we place on ourselves. Positive thinking is how we view situations. When we thing positively we see possibilities rather than limitations and what's right about a situation rather than what's wrong. Optimists are more successful in their careers and socially. They think positive thoughts and see the glass as half-full. On the other hand, pessimists think negative thoughts and see the glass as half-empty. The ABCDE technique will help you reframe situations in a more positive way. There are strategies you can undertake to make your life happy. Poor thinking habits are often the source of our unhappiness. You can improve your thinking style by substituting positive for negative thinking habits.

Positive Thinking

Positive thinking is about focusing on the things that you have rather than on the things you do not have. In other words, you see the glass as half-full rather than half-empty. It's about seeing possibilities rather than limitations. Positive thinkers are more likely to be successful than negative thinkers and they are also more likely to be happier. They are solution-oriented rather than problem-centred.

Positive thinking is different from self-delusion. Positive thinking on its own will not get you very far. It needs to be tempered with a dose of realism. Dreams are okay, but competencies and action plans must support them. John F. Kennedy dreamed of putting a man on the moon but backed it up with a huge multi-million-dollar space programme. Bill Gates dreamed of a computer in every household but then created the software to achieve it and the company to market it.

Realists anticipate and plan for problems. They believe that nothing ventured is nothing gained and that life is about challenge and solving problems. Realists accept that bad things sometimes happen and that nobody is immune from the vagaries of life. They have adopted flexible strategies to life, have created contingency plans to handle situations when they go wrong, and are able to roll with the punches. After all, the tree that bends with the breeze best weathers the storm.

Positive thinkers expect the best, prepare for the worst and shoot down the middle. They believe that negative events are once off. Just because one endeavour fails occasionally doesn't mean they all will. They thus minimise failure and put it into perspective. One may have to experience failure before succeeding. They also don't personalise failure by blaming themselves but believe they are in control and attribute the failure to external forces. At the same time they appreciate their achievements.

Optimists

Optimists think positive thoughts and expect good things to happen to them. They know that the mind moves in the direction of positive thoughts. We become what we think about. We get what we see, expect and aim for. Positive self-talk should be combined with positive action. Optimists confront problems face-on and try to solve them. Optimists are positive and persistent in the pursuit of goals. Without optimism Christopher Columbus would not have sailed west and discovered America when it was generally believed that the earth was flat. Without optimism and appropriate action Magellan would not have circumnavigated the world. Without optimism and steely determination Hillary would not have conquered Mount Everest. Without optimism and flying skills Charles Lindbergh would never have flown across the Atlantic Ocean on the first solo flight, thus opening the way for passenger and commercial flight. Without optimism and dedicated training Roger Bannister would not have broken the four-minute barrier for the mile. Without optimism, hard work and feedback from hundreds of failures Edison would not have produced the first electric light bulb.

Optimists look at the past with satisfaction and look to the future with hope. They count their blessings by cultivating an attitude of gratitude for what they have. There is always something to be thankful for.

> **"Let us all rise up and be thankful, for if we didn't learn a lot today, at least we learned a little; and if we didn't learn a little, at least we didn't get sick; and if we got sick, at least we didn't die; so, let us all be thankful."**
> **— Buddha**

Optimists refuse to put themselves down. They accept themselves for what they are and measure themselves against their own standards. They know that success is 80 per cent attitude and 20 per cent aptitude.

Optimists are more motivated at work. They have higher job performance, greater job satisfaction, better interpersonal relationships, make more money and are more likely to be innovative and playful than pessimists. Optimists experience less distress than pessimists when dealing with difficulties in their lives. They know that with hard work and determination you can overcome obstacles and achieve most things in life. Optimists respond positively to pressure. They are more emotionally stable and handle stress better. They are more flexible and stable in the face of setbacks. They are better able to handle rejection and thus make good salespeople. In practice people vary from the very optimistic to the very pessimistic, with most people falling somewhere in between.

Optimists Live Longer

Optimists think about ageing in a positive way and thus live longer. The magazine *Vibrant Life* (2002) reports that researchers at Yale University interviewed more than 600 people aged 50 and over about their attitudes on getting older. The study's participants were then followed for 23 years. Individuals with positive thoughts about ageing lived an average of 7.5 years longer than those with negative thoughts about old age. It seems that looking forward to the ageing process has as much influence on long-term survival as better-known factors such as low blood pressure and cholesterol, exercise or well-controlled weight.

Goode (2000) reports on research carried out by the Mayo Clinic in the US. They interviewed 839 people in the 1960s, and classified them, on the basis of their attitudes towards life, as optimistic or pessimistic. Thirty years later, the biographies of the 839 were examined, and it was found that those who had been labelled optimists three decades earlier lived about 19 per cent longer, probably because they were more likely to take care of themselves and were less fatalistic about their health. They also may recover faster from surgery and illness such as cancer. Positive emotions trigger the release of endorphins (natural chemicals produced by the body) that relax the cardiovascular system, and also the release of cytokines, which boost the immune system. Thus optimistic people suffer less pain when they are ill and catch colds less frequently.

Bower (2001) reports that brief autobiographies written more than 60 years ago by a group of young Catholic nuns show that positive thinking may be a matter of life or death. Those nuns who chronicled positive emotions when in their twenties have lived markedly longer than those who recounted emotionally neutral personal histories. The result, which derives from a study group with unprecedented similarity in lifestyle and social status, supports earlier evidence that expressing happiness, interest, love and other positive feelings enhances physical health. The nuns were engaging in a study conducted by Deborah D. Danner of the University of Kentucky into ageing and Alzheimer's disease. Outside convents, social status has been shown to correlate strongly with longevity, even for celebrities. Academy Award winners live an average of four years longer than actors who were nominated but didn't win one!

"The optimist proclaims that we live in the best of all possible worlds; and the pessimist fears this is true."
— James Branch Cabell

Bruce (1998) reports that heart bypass patients who were more upbeat recovered faster from surgery and felt better at five-year follow-up than pessimists who had the same operation. Goldstein (2001) reports that the University of Toronto surveyed 300 women who had been cancer-free for at least two years. They found that more than 40 per cent of the women blamed stress for the disease's onset over scientifically linked factors such as genetics and environment. The study also showed that 60 per cent believe a positive attitude has kept them healthy.

Pessimists

Pessimists think negative thoughts and expect bad things to happen to them. Research shows that the average person thinks about 50,000 thoughts a day and that 80 per cent of these thoughts are negative. So you can see the potential for damage.

When pursuing goals pessimists tend to be doubtful and hesitant. They view past events in a negative way and have a similar outlook on the future. They are inclined to put themselves down and blame others for their failures. They turn minor setbacks into catastrophes by making mountains out of molehills. They have a low frustration tolerance. This means that they get annoyed and angry easily. They think their problems are unique and fail to realise that everyone has to deal with the normal frustrations of life.

Pessimists allow their emotions to rule their brains and drain them of positive feelings. Thus they are quick to take offence at the least provocation. They find it difficult to cope with the normal put-downs, small annoyances and criticisms of life. They tend to run away from problems rather than confront them. Severe pessimism leads to ill-health, anxiety and depression. Pessimistic thinking has been linked to the constriction of blood vessels, the suppression of the immune system and poorer outcomes in serious illness. Cynicism predisposes people to stress and heart disease.

Unrealistic Optimism

Too much optimism may be bad for your health, however. Carlowe (2004) reports that research has shown that more than 50 per cent of people believe they are less likely than others to be afflicted with cancer, tooth decay or a motoring accident. Psychologists describe this phenomenon as "unrealistic optimism". Recent findings from the Royal Society of Medicine may at last give pessimists something to smile about. A paper by Australian psychologist Professor Ron Gold suggests unrealistic optimism may be causing people to ignore advice on the prevention of sexually transmitted diseases, alcoholism, smoking and obesity.

Dealing with Pessimism

The following are some strategies you can adopt to counteract pessimism:

- Feed your mind with positive thoughts. Substitute positive thoughts for negative thoughts.

- To improve your low frustration tolerance say to yourself "you win some and you lose some". Accept that life is not fair. Going through life you will have to tolerate things and people you would prefer not to. Frustration should be seen as a stimulus to change rather than a prelude to aggression.

"If you keep on saying things are going to be bad, you have a good chance of being a prophet." — Isaac Bashevis Singer

---

- Let go of excess baggage. Forgiving others for real or perceived wrongs frees you from negative feeling and lets you get on with your life.

- Associate with positive people. Your attitude is likely to get contaminated if you associate with those who moan and groan all the time.

- Keep a diary. Record your thoughts and think about them later. Ascertain what triggers your negative feelings. Try to avoid these in the future. Make a list of the things you feel good about. Thinking about these will boost your confidence.

- Get as much natural light as possible during the winter. Go for walks at mid-day when there is plenty of light. Seasonal affective disorder (SAD) caused by lack of sunshine is now accepted as a cause of depression.

- Dispute the negative thought. What are the evidence and facts supporting it? Most of our fears never materialise. Psychologists define fear as False Evidence Appearing Real. Distance yourself from the negative experience. Look for other more optimistic alternatives. Practise the ABCDE method described later on in this chapter.

- Use a distraction technique to take your mind off the negative event. Some people use a rubber band on their wrist and snap it to stop the negative thought from continuing. Others redirect their attention to more positive events. Reframe your thoughts by substituting positive for negative ones.

- Use a problem-solving approach to deal with problems. Do not run away from the reality of difficulties and problems in life by denying that they exist.

Poor Thinking Habits

If you are aware of negative thinking patterns you can take corrective action to get rid of them. You must first of all be aware of these and the damage that they can do before you can take appropriate action. Poor thinking habits can be recalled by the acronym FARSIGHTED:

- **F**iltering. You concentrate on the negative rather than the positive. You find it difficult to accept praise and worry unnecessarily about your shortcomings. A Swedish proverb says that worry gives a small thing a big shadow. Worry is like blood pressure: a certain level is healthy while too much can kill you. You focus on a single negative detail and ruminate on it exclusively and excessively. One word of criticism obliterates all the praise and positive feedback received.

- **A**ll-or-nothing thinking. You see things in black and white and as right or wrong. There are no shades of grey in-between. Learn to tolerate ambiguity. There are always different ways of looking at things and different ways of achieving end results. Perfectionists set themselves impossibly high standards and anything less than perfect is seen as failure. Success to them is being 100 per cent perfect which in reality is never achievable.

- **R**easoning emotionally. This is where the heart rules the head. You allow emotions to colour and distort the way you see things. For example, you feel angry and annoyed at the least provocation. Learn to discriminate between what you feel and what is objectively true. Know the difference between what is going on in your head and what is actually happening. To challenge your own thoughts bring logic and objectivity into the equation.

- **S**hould statements. This is where you motivate yourself by guilt such as shoulds, shouldn'ts, musts and oughts. These may have been implanted in your mind at an impression-able age by significant others such as parents or authority figures. Realise that you have a choice. Focusing too much on what you and others "should" or "must" do causes self-reproach on your part, and anger and frustration on the part of your victims. Some people feel they "must" always do well in order to please others or be a worthwhile person. In real life things need not necessarily turn out the way you hoped or expected. There is no reason why you should meet other people's expectations or other people should meet your expectations or be kind or fair to you. The only person you can control is yourself. Accept that uncertainty, frustrations and disappointments are aspects of normal liv-ing. Adopt more rational beliefs characterised by wishes, needs, wants, hopes, desires and preferences. These are more flexible and adaptable to changing events.

"The person who sends out positive thoughts activates the world around him positively and draws back to himself positive results." — Norman Vincent Peale

---

- **I**nterpretation or jumping to conclusions. There are no facts to support your negative conclusion. Two common varia-tions are mind-reading and prediction. In mind-reading you attribute reasons for the other person's behaviour that may be false. You think you know what the other person is think-ing without actually asking them. In fact, you don't really know what another person is thinking unless they tell you. In prediction you assume that things may turn out badly. Stick to the old rule, "If in doubt, check it out."

- **G**eneralisation. You generalise from a single event by using the words "always" or "never". A specific failure or negative result is generalised as an endless pattern instead of a once-off event. Just because you fail once doesn't mean you're a failure or that you're stupid. Just because one thing goes wrong doesn't mean that everything will go wrong.

- **H**old responsible. You hold yourself personally responsible for events not entirely within your control. You can only be responsible for yourself and for things within your own control. You have no control over the attitudes, opinions, actions or behaviours of others.

- **T**hinking with labels. This is where you describe an event by using colourful and emotional language. Labelling is an extreme form of all-or-nothing thinking. Instead of saying, "I made a mistake", you say to yourself, "I'm a loser". The next time you label yourself or others in some way, stop for a moment and look at the evidence to support your conclusion. On a realistic and logical basis, you will find it difficult always to find supporting grounds for your negative evaluations. Stereotyping is a form of labelling.

- **E**xaggeration. You exaggerate the significance of your problems and the size of your shortcomings, while minimising your strengths. You create the worst possible scenario in your mind and then believe that it may happen. People catastrophise by making mountains out of molehills. Learn to take the setbacks of life in your stride. The media has a built-in incentive to catastrophise news in order to sell more newspapers, magazines and TV shows. However, you don't need to do the same. For example, when reading negative news about illness, you don't have to say to yourself, "That's bound to happen to me." The good news is that catastrophic thinking is a learned behaviour and thus can be unlearned.

- **D**iscounting the positive. You belittle your achievements by saying, "Anyone could have done it." You refuse to accept compliments. Do not be afraid to take praise or credit for your accomplishments.

Happiness

Happiness is a state of mind. People experience happiness when they think pleasant thoughts most of the time. The idea that we should strive for happiness in our lives is not new. The Greek philosopher Epicurus (341–270 BC) proposed the idea that pleasure is the supreme good and main goal in life — and that only through self-restraint and moderation can people achieve true happiness. John Stuart Mill (1806–1873), Scottish philosopher and economist, argued that an act is right if it brings pleasure, and wrong if it brings pain. However, he introduced a caveat that the ultimate value is the good of society, and the guiding principle of personal conduct is the welfare of the greatest number of people. The noted nineteenth-century philosopher and psychologist William James said that happiness is reflected in the ratio of one's accomplishments to one's aspirations. This would suggest that if our expectations are too high we could become happier by lowering them. The Dalai Lama says that the only way of achieving real happiness is to make other people happy.

> **"Success is not the key to happiness. Happiness is the key to success. If you love what you are doing, you will be successful." — Albert Schweitzer**

The modern world is obsessed with physical perfection and beauty. People, especially women but also men, spend considerable sums of money on cosmetic surgery in attempts to make themselves more beautiful. The cosmetic industry is only too willing to exploit our lack of self-esteem and insecurities for profit. It is true that good-looking people are slightly happier than the rest of us. Studies show they're more popular, earn more money and are perceived as smarter and more competent by others. However, before you spend all that money on a makeover, consider the fact that true beauty radiates from within and that it is enhanced by the quality of our relationships.

Little Things Bring Happiness

It's the little mundane things in life that give us happiness. Things like going for a walk in the park, browsing in a bookstore, going to the cinema, playing games, solving a difficult problem, taking a hot bath, laughing with friends, a word of appreciation, celebrating little successes, enjoying a good meal, and going for a social drink. Ordinary pleasures are the workhorses of happiness. When people become rich and famous and pursued by the paparazzi it is the little everyday privacy, events and freedoms that ordinary people enjoy that they miss. These are the things that keep us going from one day to the next. Do the things that you enjoy doing most and you will be happy.

> **"Happiness is produced not so much by great pieces of good fortune that seldom happen as by the little advantages that occur every day." — Benjamin Franklin**

According to Marano (1994), psychologist Arthur A. Stone of the State University of New York found that the same mundane events that make us happy also keep our immune system working. A pat on the back from the boss, a compliment from our partner, a good conversation with friends — these little things boost the production of antibodies, which are the body's first line of defence against illness. On the other hand, Stone found that upsetting events — criticism from the boss — have a negative effect on the immune function. But what was most striking was that pleasurable little events have a larger and longer-lasting effect.

The J-curve

Levels of happiness vary during the day. It seems we feel happier earlier in the day and those negative events experienced during the day have a cumulative affect and lead to negative moods later in the day. Honigsbaum (2004) reports that according to Oswald, an economist at Warwick University, if you traced the trajectory of most people's happiness over time it would resemble a J-curve. People typically record high satisfaction in their early twenties. This falls steadily towards middle age, before levelling off at around 42. Most of us then grow steadily happier as we grow older, with those in their sixties expressing the highest satisfaction of all — as long as they stay healthy. As you would expect people are generally more willing to help others when they are feeling happy.

Nature versus Nurture

Honigsbaum (2004) reports that the famous 1988 study of Minnesota twins found that identical siblings reared apart were as much as 50 per cent more alike in their happiness levels than fraternal twins reared in the same household. In other words, as much as half of our capacity for happiness may be inherited. This also means that half of our capacity for happiness can be influenced by our actions. So despite the fact that genes may predispose you to unhappiness, disposition can be influenced by personal choice. You can increase your level of happiness through your own actions, regardless of your heritage.

Money and Happiness

Contrary to what most people think, money does not bring happiness. It is common sense that you can't buy real friendship, you can't buy a sense of belonging, you can't buy good health, you can't buy peace of mind, you can't buy trust and you can't buy love. What you can buy is superficial and ephemeral and not the real thing. Buddhist philosophers consider contentment the greatest form of wealth. Diener et al. (1995) reports that in a study using surveys and daily observation, the availability of material resources was nine times less important to happiness than the availability of "personal" resources such as friends and family.

The level of happiness in affluent countries has not increased in line with their wealth. Being poor does make people miserable but once basic needs are provided for, money doesn't make much difference to our level of happiness. Happiness is a state of mind. Happiness does not come from outside but comes from within and depends on how you think about your life and how you perceive the world. Some people are substituting retail therapy or the notion of "shop till you drop" for spirituality. Shopping may bolster your spirit in the short-term but material possessions will not bring you long-term happiness.

> **"Happiness is not in the mere possession of money; it lies in the joy of achievement, in the thrill of creative effort."**
> **— Franklin D. Roosevelt**

There is an old saying that your health is your wealth. Without your health you are unable to do anything. Many a millionaire would willingly give away all their wealth for good health. In some Arab cultures the symbol for wealth is the digit one followed by a large number of zeros. The symbol one represents health. Take it away and you are left with zeros.

Habituation

Layard (2003) reports that over the past 50 years we have got more affluent with better homes, more clothes, longer holidays and, above all, better health. Yet surveys show clearly that happiness has not increased in the US, continental Europe or Britain. However, it is true that within any particular society at any particular moment rich people are on average happier than poorer ones. We also know that clinical depression, assessed professionally through population surveys, has risen in most countries. Habituation is a basic psychological phenomenon. People who win the lottery experience an initial surge of happiness but after a while they become acclimatised to the idea; it becomes the norm and they finish up no happier than they were before.

The Happiness Set Point

Carlin (2005) says that the things which we expect will bring us happiness rarely do. Losing weight, getting promoted or winning a huge prize will give us a temporary feeling of happiness and then we settle back into being just as happy as we've always been. Most of us have a happiness "set point", fixed by temperament and early life experiences, which is very difficult to change. Whether you win the lottery or wind up in a wheelchair, within a year or two you generally end up just about as happy (or unhappy) as you were previously.

Use Money Wisely

Using money wisely can increase our happiness. Frank (2004) reports that there is considerable evidence that if we use an increase in our incomes simply to buy bigger houses and more expensive cars it doesn't make us happier than before. But if we use an increase in our incomes to buy more of certain intangible goods — such as eliminating a long commute or a stressful job — then the evidence paints a different picture. The less we spend on conspicuous consumption goods, the better we can improve our subjective well-being; and the more time we can devote to family and friends, to exercise, sleep, leisure, travel and other restorative activities. On the best available evidence, reallocating our time and money in these and similar ways would result in healthier, longer and happier lives.

The Relative Deprivation Principle

The relative deprivation principle says that our perceptions are affected by how we compare ourselves to others. Happiness is a function of the perceived gap between what we have and what we think others have. If we compare ourselves with those who are better off we will probably feel envy. If we compare ourselves with those who are worse off we will probably feel contented. When people finally get the promotion that they have long desired they often feel a sense of anticlimax. They forget that the pleasure is often in the process of trying to get there rather than the accomplishment of the goal. In addition, they may feel that their confidence is undermined as they now compare themselves with more capable people than heretofore.

People who attain great success in sports or athletics often find it difficult to settle down into an everyday job after experiencing the success and recognition that they once enjoyed. The "highs", the public applause, and the adrenalin surges are gone. It is unlikely that they will ever again replicate the same feelings in their lifetime.

The more we have the more we want. In life we progress from want to want. Marketing people are aware of this phenomenon and exploit our need for more and more. We buy things that we want but don't actually need. We thus clutter up our lives with things that we will never use. Ralph Waldo Emerson expressed this well when he said, "Want is a growing giant whom the coat of have was never big enough to cover."

Happiness is Good for Your Health

According to Rooney et al. (2004), researchers have found that happy people usually have high self-esteem; are optimistic, outgoing and agreeable; have close relationships; have work and leisure activities that engage their skills; have deep faith; and sleep well and exercise. Much to the surprise of many, however, age, gender, education, parenthood and physical attractiveness have little influence on happiness.

Having a meaningful, satisfying, high status and interesting job will make you happy and is more important than money. Barth (1993) reports that Oxford University psychology professor Michael Argyle found that highly paid managers are not at the zenith of happiness, but professors, scientists, pastors, doctors and lawyers are. Among unskilled workers, there is widespread dissatisfaction. Unemployment has a high correlation with dissatisfaction, apathy and fear of loss. There is a contradiction at play here. Many of us dream of a life without work and yet experience our best hours at work.

How to be Happy

We all want to be happy. The following are some practical steps you can take to increase your happiness:

- Develop good relationships with your colleagues, friends, family and acquaintances. People need social support systems to help them get through crises. Give greater priority to your relationships and friendships. Develop good communication skills and become a good listener. Murray et al. (1996) found that the core factors for a happy life are number of friends, closeness of friends, closeness of family, and relationships with co-workers and neighbours. These together account for about 70 per cent of personal happiness. It is a good strategy to develop a diversity of friendships so that if one goes sour you have others to fall back on.

- Be agreeable with others. Cheer up, inspire and encourage others. Nobody likes being around people who are obnoxious and argumentative. Glass et al. (1997) says that researchers found that adopting a positive attitude about those around you is among the most important predictors of life satisfaction. Without such attitudes we are less than half as likely to feel happy.

"Happiness comes when your work and words are of benefit to yourself and others." — Buddha

---

- Act as if you are happy. Smile and walk tall. Your physical demeanour and posture does affect your mental outlook. Everyday observation would confirm that unhappy people such as down-and-outs shuffle their feet, walk slowly with eyes cast down and slouch. Like yourself and choose to be happy. As the old song goes "you have to accentuate the positive, eliminate the negative, latch on to the affirmative, and don't mess with Mr In-between"!

- Control your life. Make sure that your day is filled with things to do. Busy people are usually happy people. A feeling that you have too much to do is much better that a feeling that you have nothing to do. As Mark Twain said, "To be busy is man's only happiness". The essentials of a happy life are something to do, someone to love and something to look forward to. Develop a wide range of hobbies and pastimes.

- Maintain a healthy lifestyle by paying attention to nutrition, diet, exercise and stress. Exercise is one road to happiness. It releases endorphins — the brain's natural painkillers. Know when it's time to work and time to play. Civilisation's greatest geniuses, from Leonardo to Einstein, have all understood the value of play. All work and no play makes Jack a dull boy and an unhealthy one as well.

"The groundwork of all happiness is health." — Leigh Hunt

- Focus on what you have rather than what you want. Compare yourself with those worse off rather than with "perfect people" presented on the media. Many young people, especially women, get depressed by comparing themselves with the perfect groomed looks and figures of models or film stars.

- Laughter is the best medicine. Use laughter to cheer yourself and others up. Try to develop a sense of humour. See the humorous side to situations. Solomon (1996) shows that in studies of hundreds of adults, happiness was related to humour. The ability to laugh, whether at life itself or at a good joke, is a great source of pleasure. Indeed, those who enjoy silly humour are one-third more likely to feel happy.

- Develop a sense of mindfulness, a way of being that puts you fully in the moment without the anxiety of regretting the past or worrying about the future all the time. Reel yourself back from the future so that the present looms large. Experience the feelings in your body and the thoughts going through your mind right now. Just observe your thoughts without engaging them or trying to control them. Don't be a prisoner of your past, like Miss Havisham in Dickens's *Great Expectations*, an embittered old spinster who, jilted on her wedding day, still wanders around her house in her wedding dress.

- Adopt the Reiki Principles. Reiki is a Japanese technique for stress reduction and relaxation. The Reiki Principles enunciated by Usui Mikao recommend: "Just for today, I will not be angry. Just for today, I will not worry. Just for today, I will do my work honestly. Just for today, I will be kind to my neighbour and every living thing. Just for today, I will give thanks for my many blessings."

- Avoid distressing situations or negative people. You don't need people in your life who make you feel bad by continually undermining you or putting you down. Unhappy people surround themselves with emotional vampires who thrive on sucking the positive feelings out of them. Instead surround yourself with positive people who cherish and support you.

- Be patient with yourself. Changing ingrained habits formed over many years can take time. Some psychologists maintain that it can take at least 21 days of constant practice to change a habit. A major change such as becoming an expert in a subject takes longer still — up to 10 years. Austin (2000) reports that 68 per cent of people who consider themselves successful say that there is at least one area of their job in which they are expert. A change in career direction may take many years of preparation. Behind every great achievement is many years of education, training, practice, persistence, discipline and self-sacrifice.

"The road to happiness lies in two simple principles: find what it is that interests you and you can do well, and when you find it, put your whole soul into it — every bit of energy and ambition and natural ability you have." — John D. Rockefeller

---

- Seek out interesting and challenging work. Do work that matters — work that contributes to the betterment of society. This is why voluntary work in a local community organisation or charity is so rewarding. If you enjoy what you do you are more likely to be successful at it. Develop a balanced lifestyle with regard for the need for rest, recuperation, recreation and relaxation.

- Pay attention to your environment and make sure it contributes to feelings of well-being. Through the news media we are being continually exposed to the most negative things in the world such as terrorism, natural disasters, tragedy and murders. This is bound to adversely affect your mood. You need to focus on what is good in the world and what is good in your life.

- Take pleasure in small successes and celebrate your achievements. Celebrating minor accomplishments will keep you happy and focused on your final goal. This reinforces the attitude that success breeds success.

- Love yourself. Accept yourself unconditionally. People who like and accept themselves feel good about life in general. Lose your self-limiting beliefs and focus on your good points. At the same time you should acknowledge your faults and do something to correct them. Develop personal qualities that are conducive to happiness such as self-esteem and positive thinking. Happiness is within your control. It comes from within rather than without.

- Help others. Most people get great satisfaction and happiness from helping others. Do an altruistic act like donating blood. Contribute to a good cause. Even millionaires who needn't work set up charitable and philanthropic ventures to make them feel that they are doing something useful. Doing good makes you feel good about yourself. It enhances your self-esteem.

- Relax for 10 minutes each day. Schedule quiet time every day. Meditation, music, a nice relaxing bath, a chat with a friend and a walk in the park are all excellent ways of winding down.

- Adopt the characteristics of happy role models. Research shows that happy people are organised, busy, like socialising, are goal-oriented and have a positive mental attitude. Adopting these behaviours will make you a happier person.

- Develop the spiritual side of your life. People with spiritual beliefs are more satisfied with their lives and live longer than those who have none.

- Music affects our mood. Listen to uplifting music to put you into a good mood. Excitement or contentment and happiness are some of the typical reactions to music.

- Choose to be happy. Abraham Lincoln said that people were just about as happy as they made up their minds to be.

"The best way for a person to have happy thoughts is to count his blessings and not his cash. There is no goal better than this one: to know as you lie on your deathbed that you lived your true life, and you did whatever made you happy." — Steve Chandler

---

ABCDE Technique

This stands for activating event, beliefs, consequences, dispute, and effectively reframe. This technique will help you challenge negative thoughts and replace them with positive ones.

- **A**ctivating event. This is related to rational or irrational beliefs. Become mindful by being aware of your thoughts. Listen to your internal dialogue or self-talk. Remember the conscious mind can only hold one thought at a time. You are therefore better off thinking about something positive and empowering rather than negative and disempowering. Think for a moment how negative thoughts can dominate your mind if they remain unchallenged. Consider a student who has done badly in an examination. The poor grade is the activating event that triggers off the negative thought.

- **B**eliefs. These will affect your interpretation of the event. It is not the event in our lives, but also our perception and interpretation of the event that causes us problems. The student's irrational belief is that, because of this bad grade, he or she is neither intelligent nor a worthwhile person.

- **C**onsequences. These may be feelings of depression, shame, sadness, anger, fear, guilt or embarrassment. In Japanese culture people may experience extreme loss of face that in some instances may lead to despair and suicide. In our less extreme example, the consequence for the student is feelings of failure, depression and anxiety connected to the exam result. This in turn could result in the student giving up classes and tests and withdrawing completely from formal academic pursuits.

"Watch your manner of speech if you wish to develop a peaceful state of mind. Start each day by affirming peaceful, contented and happy attitudes and your days will tend to be pleasant and successful." — Norman Vincent Peale

---

- **D**ispute. Use the thought-stopping technique. Say to yourself "Stop!" Clap your hands or stamp your feet at the same time, as a physical manifestation of your desire to stop thinking negatively. Some people use the rubber band method — they put a rubber band around their left wrist. When the negative thought happens they pull the rubber band and release it. The quick sharp pain reminds them to discontinue the negative thought and substitute a positive one. In addition you should question yousrself. What evidence is there to support your negative thoughts? Is there another explanation? View the issue in a logical and objective way. Consider the consequences of not giving up the belief and the benefits of doing so. In our example, the student disputes the belief that the bad grade represents incompetence or worthlessness. The first step towards being competent is to feel competent and in control. He knows that the course is very difficult and that he didn't put in sufficient time and effort. People don't realise how destructive negative thoughts can be. Remember, you can change your thoughts for the better.

- **E**ffectively reframe. This is the more effective way of thinking. Affirm a new belief. Attitudes and beliefs are learned and this means they can equally be unlearned. Substitute new thoughts for your previous ones. In our example, the student adopts a more effective belief, such as the belief that the poor grade is simply a reflection of course difficulty or inadequate preparation, rather than a measure of the student's worth as a person. The student vows to learn from his mistakes, improve his time management, set goals supported by action plans, study more effectively and increase his study time for the future and do better the next time round. He affirms the belief "I can do it".

Summary

Positive thinking is about focusing on the things you have rather than the things you don't have. It's about seeing possibilities rather than limitations. It's about being solution-oriented rather than problem-centred.

Optimists know that the mind moves in the direction of our positive thoughts. We become what we think about all day long. Optimists look to the past with satisfaction and look to the future with hope.

Pessimists think negatively about the past and about the future. They are inclined to put themselves down, refuse to accept personal responsibility and blame others for their failures. There are some strategies you can adopt to counteract pessimism including feeding your mind with positive thoughts and associating with positive people.

Poor thinking habits include filtering and all-or-nothing thinking. Happiness strategies include developing good social support systems and having realistic goals. The ABCDE technique will help you reframe negative situations in a positive way.

FIVE STEPS TO IMPROVING POSITIVE THINKING

1. Make sure that your positive thinking is realistic and supported by positive action. If you want something to happen then you've got to make it happen.

2. Consider the practical steps you can take to increase your happiness. Write down the ones that appeal most to you. Gradually incorporate these behaviours into your lifestyle over the next few weeks and reflect on the results.

3. Develop a high tolerance level for frustration and discomfort and learn to cope effectively with the ups and downs of life without getting unduly distressed. Do not blow things out of proportion and keep things in perspective. Accept that things will not always go your way and that everybody you meet will not necessarily be compatible with you.

4. Consider the poor thinking habits discussed in the chapter. Reflect on those relevant to your situation and gradually eliminate them from your thinking patterns.

5. When confronted with negative thoughts practise the ABCDE method. Learn this method thoroughly so that it becomes an automatic response for dealing with negative thoughts.

Case Study: The Power of Positive Thinking

Jane is proud of the current success of her IT company called IT Works, which she set up about 15 years ago shortly after graduating with a BSc in computer science. It was not always so. It took many years of discovery, difficulties, frustration, trial and error, and determination but Jane has confirmed what she always believed to be true — with positive thinking, hard work and persistence, anything is possible. The word "can't" is not in Jane's vocabulary. She believes if you focus too much on the obstacles that you will miss the opportunities.

She is now CEO of her own company, which has lucrative contracts with some of the major multinationals and government departments in the country. In the early years there were many occasions when the company was near bankruptcy but Jane refused to quit and never lost her self-belief that she was going to succeed. In fact, at one stage she had mortgaged her house to fund the company. This showed total commitment to her goals, as there was only one acceptable outcome at this stage — success.

Jane is very organised and surrounds herself with good capable people. IT Works now employs 20 people and Jane prides herself on her good interpersonal relationship and leadership skills and is a good motivator of people. She is also good at motivating herself. She keeps in touch with what is going on through regular weekly meetings and her leadership style of "management by wandering about". Five years ago she returned to college on a part-time basis and completed a Masters degree in information technology. She used the knowledge and expertise acquired on the course to improve and expand the services her company offered. She also made many friends and good business contacts while doing the programme.

As a positive and optimistic person, Jane has attracted similar people into IT Works. Jane's optimism and enthusiasm is contagious. She believes that the difficulty a lot of people have is that they are reluctant to put in the work necessary to achieve success. She finds that some people get frustrated when they do not achieve success quickly. Her favourite quote is, "The average overnight success takes about 15 years", which proved to be very true in her own case.

Jane believes in networking and is a member of the local computer society. This gives her an opportunity to meet like-minded people and is also occasionally a source of business. Jane has also encouraged her staff to get actively involved in the society. Jane believes in working very hard when the occasion warrants it and expects her staff to do likewise. At the same time she acknowledges the need for rest and recreation. She believes in celebrating success. New contracts and the successful completion of existing contracts are all occasions for celebration with staff. Consequently, Jane has built up a great team spirit within her company. She believes that her staff should share in the success of the company that they have helped her build up and has made them shareholders in the company. This has given staff an inherent interest in the company and has made many of them, including herself, fairly wealthy.

Jane loves the challenge of being an entrepreneur and making use of the knowledge and expertise that she had developed in IT. Jane has always believed in her own creativity and has proved this in the novelty of the IT solutions she has come with over the years. She also encourages her staff to be creative. She loves being in control of her own destiny and loves the flexibility the business gives her. She is confidently looking forward to another 15 years of continued success in the business.

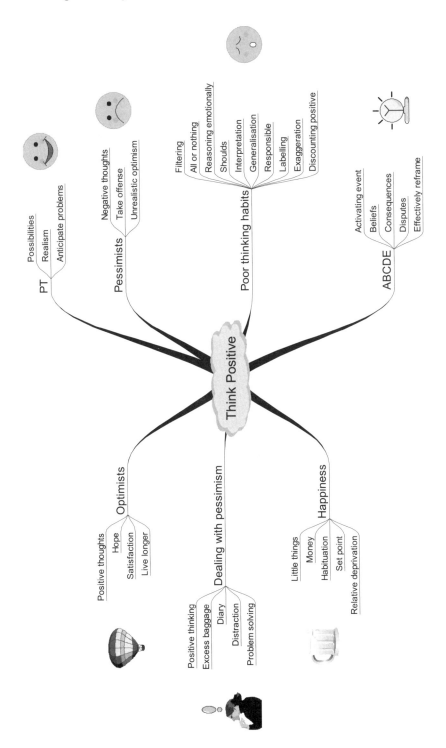

Think Positive

PT
- Possibilities
- Realism
- Anticipate problems

Pessimists
- Negative thoughts
- Take offense
- Unrealistic optimism

Poor thinking habits
- Filtering
- All or nothing
- Reasoning emotionally
- Shoulds
- Interpretation
- Generalisation
- Responsible
- Labelling
- Exaggeration
- Discounting positive

ABCDE
- Activating event
- Beliefs
- Consequences
- Disputes
- Effectively reframe

Optimists
- Positive thoughts
- Hope
- Satisfaction
- Live longer

Dealing with pessimism
- Positive thinking
- Excess baggage
- Diary
- Distraction
- Problem solving

Happiness
- Little things
- Money
- Habituation
- Set point
- Relative deprivation

9

IMPROVEMENT

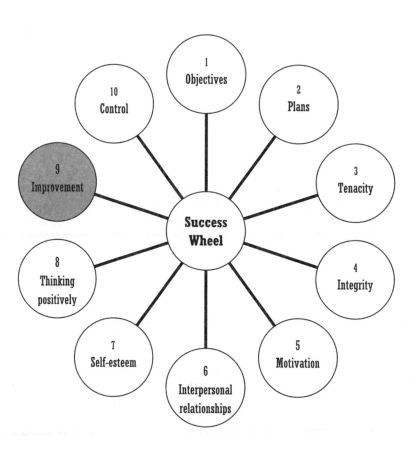

♦ What is lifelong learning?

♦ What is the change process?

♦ What do I need to know about learning?

♦ How can I keep mentally fit?

♦ What are the learning stereotypes about older learners?

♦ What is peak performance?

"There is only one thing that will really train the human mind and that is the voluntary use of the mind by the man himself. You may aid him, you may guide him, you may suggest to him and, above all else, you may inspire him. But the only thing worth having is that which he gets by his own exertions, and what he gets is in direct proportion to what he puts in." — Albert L. Lowell

---

I stands for improvement (as in learning and development) and is the ninth letter of our acronym OPTIMISTIC. Knowing something about the change process will help you manage change more effectively. Continuous improvement and learning is one of the keys to success in this life. Growth and self-actualisation should be our aim. We need to update our existing knowledge and skills and acquire new knowledge and skills as long as we live. As well as keeping physically fit we must keep mentally fit as well. The brain is a marvellous machine but most of us get no instruction in how to use it. There is now more knowledge about the brain and how people learn and we can use this knowledge to make us more effective learners and more successful people. Learning to learn skills are the key to the future. We can continue to learn and develop successfully as we age, provided we challenge ourselves mentally.

Change

We have two choices as regards change. We can embrace it enthusiastically and benefit from it or we can resist change and get run over. Change is a constant, natural and inevitable part of life. It happens whether we like it or not. Change is not a modern invention. It has always been part and parcel of life. The seasons change cyclically from winter to spring to summer to autumn and back to winter again. We continually change ourselves. We go through a biological life cycle. We are born, grow up, mature and eventually decline and die. In addition the world around us is continually changing. The only thing that is different is the speed of modern change.

The key ingredient is our attitude towards change. One side of human nature resists change and craves for peace and quiet, while another side welcomes novelty and excitement. All progress is facilitated by change. If we have the courage to embrace change we will grow and develop through new challenges and experiences. If we ignore change we will stagnate and be left behind. It would be wrong to assume that all change is good. Worthwhile change brings benefits. Unnecessary change may bring problems and hardship.

The Change Stages

People can become more capable of handling change and more resilient to handling disappointment if they understand the natural change process most people go through when they are confronted with major change in their lives such as divorce, bereavement and redundancy. It is comforting to know that most people go through some or all of the same stages. These changes, which are based on the work of Elisabeth Kubler-Ross on death and dying, can be described as follows:

- *Denial*. Our first reaction is to resist or deny that change is happening. We refuse to accept reality. In the case of bereavement we may fantasise that our loved one is still alive. We feel helpless and powerless. This avoidance approach may help you cope with the problem in the short term but can be detrimental in the long term.

- *Anger*. Your sense of shock and disbelief is now replaced with anger. We are angry at God or at the world that he has allowed this terrible thing to happen. We are even angry with the deceased person for leaving us alone in the world. We feel we are being treated unfairly and haven't done anything to deserve this. We are traumatised and out of control.

- *Negotiation*. We try to bargain or negotiate a deal to reverse the process of change so that we can resume where we started and regain some control over the situation. We may bargain with God that if he reverses the situation we will reform our lives. When we realise that this will not happen we begin to get depressed.

- *Depression*. Reality has set in. There is a sense of mourning at the loss suffered. We feel our loved one has gone forever and have concerns about how we are going to cope with the future without them.

- *Options*. Alternatives are now considered and consequences evaluated. We begin to realise that we can bounce back from this setback. There are people in worse situations than you. You get off your butt, brush yourself off and start all over again or alternatively descend into the abyss of morbidity. Most people go for the first choice.

- *Acceptance*. We stop feeling sorry for ourselves. We realise that life goes on irrespective of our loss. We accept that death is a natural part of life. We are grateful for the good times and fond memories. We now adopt a more positive attitude, get on with our lives and plan for the future.

In modern life we must be able to cope with change and turn it to our advantage. One way of doing this is by taking up the challenge of lifelong learning.

Lifelong Learning

Changes in work organisation and management, such as delayering, outsourcing, multiskilling and flexible working, combined with more focus on markets, competition, consumption and lifestyles, has made lifelong learning the new imperative. In the information age, the rapid rate of technological change means we have to update our learning and skills throughout our working lives. To survive in the workplace you need numerate skills, financial literacy skills, writing skills, communication skills, negotiation skills, presentation skills, interpersonal relationship skills as well as computer skills. Improve your personal efficiency by developing problem-solving skills, creativity skills, speed-reading skills, memory skills and mind-mapping skills. Study the principles of successful living as laid out in this book. Many training organisations provide short courses in these and other personal development areas. Listen to motivational and personal development tapes and CDs.

"We have an innate desire to endlessly learn, grow and develop. You want to become more than you already are. Once we yield to this inclination for continuous and never-ending improvement, we lead a life of endless accomplishments and satisfaction." — Chuck Gallozzi

---

Lifelong learning is thus now the norm. To earn more we've got to learn more. We are continually learning, on-the-job and off-the-job. Indeed we must continually update our skills just to keep our existing job. In addition to skills, we also need more general knowledge and social skills to equip us to deal with the demands of the modern workplace and the demands of modern living. Many people even change professions during a lifetime and this will involve substantial re-training, education and learning. An attitude of continuous learning and improvement is essential for survival in the modern world.

People now undertake study and new learning experiences at all stages of their life cycle. The days when you could throw away the books after leaving college are long gone. People are pursuing specialist qualifications at diploma, degree and post-graduate level to develop them and improve their prospects of promotion and advancement in their jobs. The internet has opened up the possibilities of further education without having to leave the comfort of your own home. Most third-level colleges now offer qualifications that you can study for at night. The range of learning opportunities available is now almost limitless. There is something available to meet all interests and needs.

Research has established that on average the more edu-cated you are the longer you will live and the healthier you will be. Part of the explanation seems to be that highly educated people earn more, and know more, and are thus more likely to adopt healthy lifestyles. Because of their higher incomes they eat more nutritious food and also can access better health re-sources. They are less likely to become obese. More highly educated people are also likely to finish up in jobs where they have greater control. Lack of control over your life is a well-known source of stress.

The Brain and Learning

Knowing how our brain works will help us become better life-long learners. Most of us know very little about the amazing computer in our heads. When you buy a computer you get an instruction manual on how to use it. However, we come into the world with no idea of how to use our brain which is the most ad-vanced and sophisticated computer in the world. The following are a few useful things to know about the brain and learning:

- Learning is influenced by emotions. Confidence, self-esteem, expectancy, our need for social approval, biases, prejudices, attitudes and beliefs, all influence our capacity to learn. Enthusiasm for a subject and self-efficacy is the best foundation for learning.

- We learn at both conscious and subconscious levels simultaneously. Suggestology, on which accelerated learning is built, is based on the theory that suggestions can and do affect the outcome of learning. Thus a supportive environment and encouragement can enhance our ability to learn.

- Learning is enhanced by challenge and inhibited by threat. Tasks that are too difficult may frustrate learners. Tasks that are too easy may not retain their interest and commitment. Thus we need to be stretched a little to learn effectively.

- The brain is designed to perceive and generate patterns. Learning is an active dynamic process of constructing meaning through the use of patterns. The brain loves to complete jigsaw puzzles and do crosswords but must be provided with meaningful pieces or clues to do so — it resists meaningless patterns or clues. It is thought that the reason why mind maps are so useful is that they mimic the pattern-seeking organisation of the brain. Neuroscientists believe that learning occurs through a change in the strength of certain synaptic connections in the brain. A frequently used synapse may grow stronger, whereas an infrequently used synapse will grow weaker and even disappear over time. This means that repetition and frequent practice are essential for learning. Develop learning-to-learn skills.

- Learning is a holistic phenomenon. The mind affects the body and the body affects the mind. Stress management, psychological support, nutrition, ventilation, exercise, rest and relaxation are important ingredients in the whole learning process. So take periodic breaks for rest and reflection when learning.

- The brain has two halves, called hemispheres. The right side is the artistic side and the left side is the scientific side. The two sides work together and interact all the time, whether a person is dealing with words, maths, music, or art. Learning is cumulative and developmental. Learning must be put in context for meaning. Some people are more left-brained and logical than right-brained and creative and vice versa. Develop those parts of the brain that you currently under-utilise. If you are a very logical person try to develop your creative side.

- The search for meaning and purpose in our lives is an innate requirement for humans. We all need to make sense of the world. Just as the body needs nutrition, the brain needs challenging information. Learning is most effective in a stimulating and supportive environment. When learning you should focus on meaning and understanding rather than rote memorisation.

- Learning involves concentration and peripheral vision. Information is transmitted to the subconscious brain through visual and verbal cues. Engage all your senses — visual, verbal and tactile — when learning.

"Become addicted to constant and never-ending self-improvement." — Anthony J. D'Angelo

---

- Activity-based learning is remembered better and longer than any other type of learning. Hence you remember better what you do and say. This means that on-the-job learning is the most effective.

- Our brains may be similar in many ways but they are moulded uniquely by different genetic, cultural and life experiences. The brain is flexible and learning changes its structure. The more we learn, the more developed and complex our brain becomes. In Wernicke's area of the brain, which deals with word understanding, the nerve cells have more dendrites in university-educated people than in people with only a secondary education. The brain is like a muscle; the more we use it the better it becomes.

Multiple Intelligence

The theory of multiple intelligence should boost your confidence about your innate ability to learn whatever you want. It is now thought that conventional IQ only accounts for about 10 per cent of our success in life. Emotional, social and practical intelligence are now thought to be more important. We have many intelligences, so many in fact that we won't have the time necessary to develop all of them in a lifetime. However, through specialisation we can become expert in some. What is your particular gift? We all have some gift that we should exploit for our advantage. The following intelligences are based on Howard Gardner's theory of multiple intelligence:

- *Linguistic*. You are good at language; you like words and stories and are very good at expressing yourself. People with this gift become writers, actors, broadcasters and publishers. Others just like telling a good story.

- *Mathematical*. You like mathematics, are good at calculations and solving abstract problems. People with this gift become scientists, mathematicians and accountants. Others just like solving logic puzzles.

"What is important is to keep learning, to enjoy challenge, and to tolerate ambiguity. In the end there are no certain answers." — Martina Horner
---

- *Visual*. You like looking at pictures, diagrams, maps, illustrations and you have a good eye for colour. People with this gift become architects, artists and illustrators. Other just like to sketch.

- *Physical*. You like sport and physical exercise. You like to be up and about and move all the time. People with this gift become footballers, athletes and dancers. Others just like to go hill walking.

- *Musical*. You like all kinds of music and listening to music can influence your mood. People with this gift become musicians, composers and singers. Others just like to whistle to a good tune or listen to their favourite CDs.

- *Emotional*. You know how to manage and control your emotions. You understand how other people feel. People with this gift become psychologists, psychiatrists, social workers and counsellors. Others just like to help people.

- *Social.* You enjoy the company of other people. You like working in teams and helping other people solve problems. People with this gift become diplomats, facilitators and social workers. Others just like to spend time with good friends.

- *Environmental.* You like living in and observing the natural world. You notice things that others miss. People with this gift become environmentalists, farmers and foresters. Others just like being in the countryside, taking walks in the forest and enjoying nature.

- *Spiritual.* You are concerned with the meaning of life; why we are put on this earth, and where we are going. People with this gift become philosophers, priests and ministers of religion. Others just enjoy contemplating the mysteries of life.

- *Practical.* You have a hands-on approach to problems. You enjoy finding solutions to everyday problems and are a keen DIY person. Common sense is a type of practical intelligence. People with this gift become mechanics, carpenters, electricians and plumbers. Others just like solving problems with their hands.

Learning Effectively

Being aware of the learning cycle and learning styles will help us learn more effectively. The learning cycle corresponds with doing something (activist), reflecting or thinking about it (reflector), understanding and concluding (theorist), and then doing it differently (pragmatist). It is similar to the continuous improvement cycle of plan, do, check and act. Thus the four learning styles are derived from the learning cycle and are activist, reflector, theorist and pragmatist.

1. *Activist.* Activists enjoy getting things done. They enjoy learning new experiences even if they have little practical value. They like variety, excitement and action. They are very much involved in the here and now. They tend not to reflect on what they are about to do or consider future consequences.

2. *Reflector.* Reflectors think deeply about their experiences and consider them from different viewpoints. They like to

consider facts before arriving at a conclusion. They tend to be cautious and have a "look before you leap" attitude.

3. *Theorist*. Theorists are rational and logical and keen on basic assumptions, principles, concepts, theorems, models and systems. They like to be intellectually stretched. They try to organise different facts into coherent theories.

4. *Pragmatist*. Pragmatists are practitioners and doers rather than thinkers. They are more concerned that ideas, theories and techniques work in practice. They are only interested in things that have a practical application.

Consider the four learning styles. Which one do you think closely resembles your style of learning? In fact, most of us have a little of all styles in our makeup. However, we probably are dominant in one or two styles. You may wish to develop those styles that you are currently weak in.

Making the Most of Your Memory

A good memory is the basis of all learning. Psychologists have proved that you can improve your memory by exercising well-known memory skills. It is now generally accepted that the memory process is facilitated if:

- The information is of relevance and interest to the learner and put to immediate use. Things are remembered even better if you are emotionally interested in the topic.

- An item to be committed to memory is repeated and practised. Spaced practice is best rather than repetition in one intense session.

- Items to be committed to memory are linked, connected, and associated with existing knowledge and experience. Consciously link new knowledge with existing knowledge and everyday life experiences.

- The item to be committed to memory comes first, or last, in the sequence. This is known as the *Primacy* and *Recency* principle. Primacy means we remember better what we did first rather than what came subsequently. Recency means we remember better what we did last or most recently.

- Getting an overview of a topic facilitates subsequent learning. Hence the value of mind maps and chapter summaries.

- The information is immediately meaningful — learning such information takes about one-tenth of the effort to learn than comparable information that makes no sense.

- You concentrate on the key points or important issues. The average short-term memory has a capacity of between five and nine items. By concentrating on key points you are applying this principle.

- You use your powers of visual imagination by visualising pictures in your head. Experience the feelings and sensations in your mind to make them more memorable.

- You continually challenge your mind by learning new subjects and developing new skills, so developing and extending the neural connections in the brain. Use it or lose it should be your guiding principle.

- You are relaxed when learning. It is impossible to pay attention if you are tense or anxious. Psychologists have discovered that constant exposure to stress kills off brain cells and causes memory loss. To learn effectively you need to be challenged but not overwhelmed.

- Use mnemonic and acronym devices as appropriate to help you associate facts with images. Research has proved that people who consciously use mnemonic and acronym devices for organising and remembering things do better at recall than those who don't. These devices force you to concentrate on what you want to remember.

Ageing and the Brain

Johnson (2000) reports that one of the most fundamental research findings of the 1990s — "the decade of the brain" — is that neurons and their interconnections can remain remarkably plastic into one's eighties and beyond. The brain is not a preset, unalterable network of cells. Ageing connections can remain flexible, and new ones can even be formed, regardless of how old that grey matter becomes. This is extremely important because it indicates that the brain can reroute connections around areas that may be growing old, rigid with age or even bring back those areas to greater functionality.

"The greatest potential for growth and self-realisation exists in the second half of life." — Carl Jung

---

There are reams of evidence that old people who stay in touch with family, friends, church and society stay in better shape physically and mentally. Data even show that an active social life benefits brain function as much as physical exercise does. Staying socially active also helps maintain a positive attitude and a good self-image, by improving feelings of self-worth. One study showed that older adults who attended religious services at least once a week lived longer than those who did not.

Physical and Mental Exercise

Scientists are only beginning to understand how we can maintain our brain's plasticity. Physical exercise is one. The physical exertion of the cardiovascular and muscular systems seems to keep the brain more pliable. One study shows that aerobic walking improves executive function in people between the ages of 60 and 75, and there is no reason to believe that this would not hold true for 80- to 90-year-olds. The subjects' ability to switch rapidly from one task to another improved, their distractibility decreased, and their ability to stop doing whatever they were doing (such as taking their foot off the accelerator while driving) increased.

The most important way of maintaining brain plasticity is mental exercise. The ageing brain is just as powerful in learning as younger brains. The old phrase, "You can't teach an old dog new tricks" is simply not true. Mental challenges, from crossword puzzles to political debates with friends, keep neuronal connections strong, just as physical exercise keep the body strong. Undertaking completely new hobbies, vocations, or intellectual pursuits can help even further. Learning in old age may take longer, but we remain potential learners our entire lives.

How to Age-proof Your Mind

Scientists now believe that the decline in mental effectiveness as we age can be slowed down or even reversed. The following is a synopsis of what they advise:

- Don't retire from life. Keep actively involved in something you have a passion for. You may retire from a job but you should never retire from life. Retire from something, not from everything.

"Don't ever think of retiring from the world until the world will be sorry that you retire. I hate a fellow whom pride or cowardice or laziness drive into a corner, and does nothing when he is there but sit and growl. Let him come out as I do, and bark." — Samuel Johnson

---

- Set and reset goals throughout your life so that you have something meaningful and purposeful to live for. Look forward to the future with optimism and anticipation.

- Don't resist change. Adopt and adapt to new technological developments. Sherer (1996) found that the self-esteem and life satisfaction of senior citizens who learned how to use personal computers increased by 5 per cent. If you have difficulty setting up your DVD player or your mobile phone your grandchild will show you how to do it.

- Watch your diet and stay physically fit.

- Become an expert in something. Research and read widely on your chosen topic.

- Learn to take the trials and tribulations of life in your stride.

- Do crossword puzzles or take up bridge.

- Go out with your friends and make new friends. Lawson (2005) reports that people who have many friends and who spend a large amount of time with them live longer than those with fewer social outlets, according to a study of elderly adults. Researchers found no link between longevity and time spent with family. Over the course of 10 years the most socially connected of subjects were 22 per cent less likely to die than people who had few close friends and little social contact. Researchers speculate that close friends help their companions stay on top of physical and emotional problems.

- Turn off the TV and read instead. This will challenge your mind and keep you mentally alert. Apart from anything else TV may give you a distorted and negative view of life.

- Keep interested in current affairs. This will give you plenty to talk about.

- Live an interesting life. Travel abroad and see the world.

- Keep a diary as something to pass on to your children and grandchildren.

The Flow Zone

When we do what we enjoy doing the most we are more likely to get "in the zone" and experience "flow". Athletes who win sometimes state that prior to their success they were in the zone, an emotional state of total relaxation, concentration, calmness and confidence. Psychologist Mihalyi Csikszentmihalyi (1991) suggests that optimal learning occurs when you achieve your "flow" state of concentration. This is a distinctive state of mind and feeling in which learning is effortless and enjoyable. The flow is also known as the stretch zone (see the next chapter) because it takes you out of your comfort zone.

In the flow zone you will learn more, acquire new skills, increase your self-esteem and self-confidence and equip yourself to take on even more challenging work. In this zone you have the energy and confidence to keep going. This is the zone you're in when you are learning new skills that excite your passion and engage your imagination. Absorbing hobbies will engage your imagination and put you into the flow zone.

Csikszentmihalyi has studied the conditions which give rise to a state of flow. He concludes that a state of flow is achieved when:

- The challenge is just slightly greater than the skill required to achieve it.

- Clear goals have been established.

- Feedback is immediate.

- There is no concern about possible failure.

When these conditions are met, the attention on the task becomes focused and fully engaged, and the passage of time may literally be forgotten.

Summary

Knowing something about the change process will help you manage the change in your life more effectively. Changes in work organisation and management have made lifelong learning the new imperative. People now undertake study and new learning experiences at all stages of their life cycle. We are in fact biological learning machines and goal-seeking mechanisms consciously and subconsciously learning all the time.

Knowing how our brain works will help us become better lifelong learners. Proficiency in learning-to-learn skills will make you a more effective learner. When you buy a computer, you get an instruction manual on how to use it. However, we come into the world with no idea on how to use our brain, which is the most sophisticated and advanced computer in the world.

Knowledge of the theory of multiple intelligence will boost our confidence and self-belief by making us aware of the amazing abilities we have waiting to be exploited. Learning styles will make you conscious of the fact that we all learn in different ways and may have dominant ways of doing so. Memory is the basis of learning. Psychologists have proved that you can improve your memory by exercising well-known memory skills.

There is no reason why we can't learn new skills as we grow older. The myth that you can't teach an old dog new tricks has long been put to rest. Peak performance is experienced by those who do what they enjoy doing most. Optimal learning occurs when you achieve the "flow" state of concentration.

FIVE STEPS TOWARDS PERSONAL IMPROVEMENT

1. **Reflect on the change model and realise that most people go through some or all of these change stages. Overlearn the model so that it becomes part of your subconscious. Forewarned is forearmed so this model should save you from any "surprises" you may experience when going through any change process. You are thus in a position to proactively prepare for them.**

2. **Draw up a lifelong learning plan. Consider what you will set out to learn over the next year and up to five years ahead. Revise your lifelong learning plan at the end of each year in preparation for the next year. Consider the action steps you will need to undertake to bring your plan to fruition.**

3. **Classify your abilities using the Multiple Intelligence Model. Consider those that would be advantageous for you to develop further to improve your life skills and enhance your career prospects.**

4. **Consider the points about improving your memory. Gradually adopt those that appeal to you into an everyday memory improvement plan. Memory is like a muscle; the more you use it the better it becomes.**

5. **Reflect on the points raised about the brain and learning. Incorporate those that you consider the most useful into your lifestyle.**

Case Study: Lifelong Learning

Bill always believed in the idea of lifelong learning. Throughout his life he has continued to challenge himself by undertaking new learning experiences as he progressed in his career. He left secondary school in 1972 with an honours leaving certificate. His parents had died before he completed his education so he was very much on his own. He had ambitions of going to university but this was out of the question as the expense involved was too high. He had no option but to go and work for a living.

He eventually got a job with a large multinational company that had an educational support scheme for those willing to study on a part-time basis. On enquiry he found that he could study cost and management accountancy without being indentured, provided he got the appropriate experience while working.

Bill decided to study for the qualification by correspondence course. The qualification took five years' intense study to complete but at the end of the process Bill got his "letters" and was now a professionally qualified accountant. Shortly after qualifying Bill was offered a promotional position in the company's internal audit department, which he took up. This involved doing internal audit investigations in the company's departments and various plants throughout the company. This was excellent experience and was considered a good route to a senior management position within the company. After four years as an internal auditor Bill was promoted again but this time into the Management Services area. This involved doing operational research, work study, and efficiency studies throughout the organisation. During this time he decided to do further study and qualified within three years as an industrial engineer. This involved night classes at the local third-level college.

Within another four years Bill was offered a senior management position in the Personnel Department of the company. A firm believer in lifelong learning Bill now decided to do an MSc in behavioural science which was a two-year part-time programme at a local college. The programme involved written exams and a thesis of 25,000 words in the final year. In two years Bill had completed his degree with distinction. Four years later Bill applied for and got the job as the Human Resource Director of the company. Through-

out his career Bill had changed professions but each time he made sure that he acquired the necessary knowledge and skill to help him do the job efficiently and effectively. Bill now encourages people throughout the company to become lifelong learners.

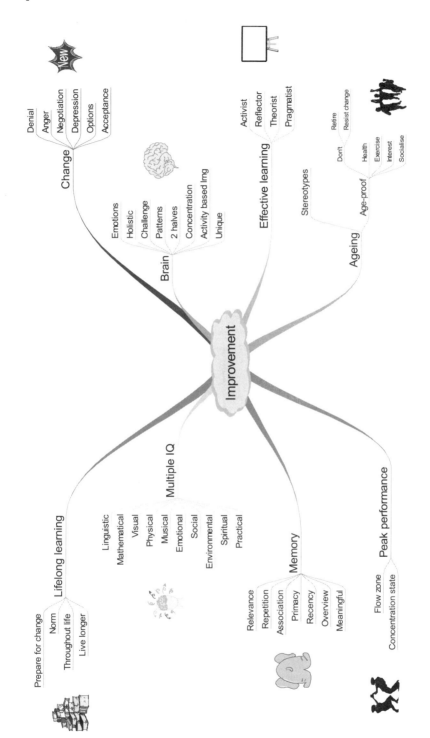

Improvement

Change
- Denial
- Anger
- Negotiation
- Depression
- Options
- Acceptance

Brain
- Emotions
- Holistic
- Challenge
- Patterns
- 2 halves
- Concentration
- Activity based Img
- Unique

Effective learning
- Activist
- Reflector
- Theorist
- Pragmatist

Ageing
- Stereotypes
- Age-proof
  - Dont
    - Retire
    - Resist change
  - Health
    - Exercise
    - Interest
    - Socialise

Lifelong learning
- Prepare for change
  - Norm
  - Throughout life
  - Live longer

Multiple IQ
- Linguistic
- Mathematical
- Visual
- Physical
- Musical
- Emotional
- Social
- Environmental
- Spiritual
- Practical

Memory
- Relevance
- Repetition
- Association
- Primacy
- Recency
- Overview
- Meaningful

Peak performance
- Flow zone
- Concentration state

10

CONTROL

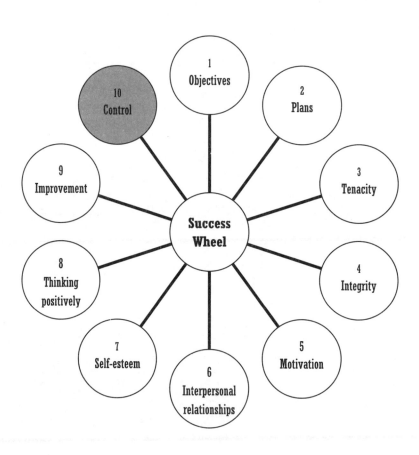

- ♦ Why is self-discipline important to success?
- ♦ How can I achieve work–life balance?
- ♦ What is the locus of control?
- ♦ What is the comfort zone?
- ♦ How can I use time management principles to help me?
- ♦ Why is financial discipline so important to success?

"What we do upon some great occasion will probably depend on what we already are; and what we are will be the result of previous years of self-discipline." — H. P. Liddon

---

C is for control and is the last letter of our acronym OPTIMISTIC. Control or self-discipline is about managing your life effectively. Many people achieve all the success in the world but somehow manage to throw it all away. Through lack of self-discipline they over-indulge in food, drink, drugs, sex and other excesses. Many die before their time.

Those of us with more mundane jobs often lack the self-discipline of living within our means and finish up overwhelmed with debt. Lack of financial discipline is a major source of stress in many people's lives. In our work lives some of us become workaholics and fail to adopt a healthy work–life balance. In our relationships we are unable to control our emotions and create unhappiness and resentment to those around us. In our personal lives some of us enter into extra-marital relationships putting our home and family lives and even our health at risk. Many of us fail to practise basic time management skills so that our lives are disorganised and wasteful. Some of us are not masters of our own destiny but rather victims of circumstance and whim.

Self-discipline

This is a world of instant self-gratification, materialism and selfishness. In the modern world we have instant coffee, instant meals and instant cash from automatic tellers. The shops are open 7 days a week and some 24 hours a day. We are used to having our needs satisfied instantly. To many, money is freely available and appears to be no object. Get it now and pay later is the motto. The modern world is built on credit. We are tempted on every side and facilitated with credit cards and a consumerist mentality to live beyond our means. The idea of postponing gratification and doing without in the present and saving for future needs has gone out of fashion. We are constantly bombarded by advertisements to buy things that we want but don't really need.

An important aspect of self-discipline is emotional control. We are governed by our emotions. Modern examples of when people are emotionally out of control include road rage and air rage. To be successful in life you need to be in control of your moods and emotions. Negative feelings like spite, anger, jealousy, resentment, hatred, hostility, envy and revenge must be kept in check. In particular, resenting others' good luck, wealth, success or talent is counterproductive. Continuous resentment may cause you to become ill. Some people think that disease can be a physical manifestation of resentment. Resentment is an emotional response to circumstances and is therefore within your control. Resentment often means playing the same old negative thoughts over and over again. Choose not to do so.

You also need to be able to control the stress in your life. Successful people have a high level of emotional maturity, introspection and social skills. Being in control of your emotions means that you can postpone gratification and stifle impulsive behaviour. People with self-discipline can plan for the future and diligently pursue their dreams and goals with hard work and persistence over many years. They sacrifice the present for future gain.

"Discipline is the bridge between goals and accomplishments." — Jim Rohn

---

A perception of being in control of your situation may be good for your health. Agrawal et al. (2001) found that when cardiac patients blamed God for their disease they showed poor physical recovery, and their mood was less positive. When the patients blamed themselves for the onset of the cardiac disease, physical recovery was better, and there was a more positive mood and perception of recovery. Those who attribute their illness to factors under their personal control have been found to initiate active efforts toward recovery and toward preventing recurrence of the disease, for example, by engaging in more healthy behaviour. Efforts to enhance a sense of control in cardiac patients have been found in other studies to be beneficial.

People who can't control their emotions often cause the breakdown of friendships and marriages. People say things on the spur of the moment causing deep hurt that they later regret. Unfortunately it is then too late. Words said in the heat of the moment cannot be taken back. People should think before they speak and consider the consequences of what they say. In the work context, conflict and industrial relations problems are often caused by heated verbal exchanges. The exercise of good communication and interpersonal relationship skills would avert the problem.

Work–Life Balance

Many people are overwhelmed with work and desire a better lifestyle. Some are working 40 to 60 hours per week and spending an additional 10 to 20 hours commuting. Many workers are exhausted and stressed from juggling too many responsibilities. As well as looking after their own children many also have the added responsibility of looking after ageing parents. They feel their lives are out of control. They want to have more leisure time and time for their families. Some are even prepared to take a job with lower responsibilities and lower salary to meet their goal.

Downshifting is now the priority for many people. They are tired of the excessive consumption, selfishness and materialism of modern living and are prepared to sacrifice some of the excesses for a simpler and more meaningful life. Downshifting is where people exchange their work status for more flexibility and free time. Downshifting suits older and unattached workers who find it easier than younger people with a family to support.

Professional workers will often have less difficulty than factory workers in switching to self-employment. Information technology has made it easier for many professionals to work from home. Different people have different priorities but most of us want to find some purpose and meaning in life besides being consumed by work. They realise the need to slow down to avoid stress, workaholism and burnout. Material wealth is no good if your health declines and you can't enjoy life. When making decisions people should have regard to the impact the decision will have on different aspects of their lives.

Different Work Arrangements

In response to the need to downshift, employers have invented unique approaches to flexible working. Being aware of these possible options may help you make a more informed decision if you want to downshift. These include part-time working, job sharing, flexitime, annualised hours, term-time working, compressed working week, reduced working hours and teleworking or home-working.

Part-time work is where the hours of work are arranged to suit both the employer and the employee. Job-sharing is where two employees share one full-time position. The work is divided equally between the two, perhaps splitting the working day or week. Term-working is where an employee works one week on and another week off. A compressed working week is where the employee works the full number of hours in a reduced number of days, such as working a four-day week.

Flexitime provides the worker with flexible starting and finishing times. Annualised hours are where a part-time or full-time employee works a set number of hours over a year, with the hours arranged to suit the employer and worker. Teleworking means working from home using information and communication technologies that are linked to the office. They all involve compromise and some involve a reduction in salary but people are prepared to make the sacrifice in order to live a more stress-free life.

Most dual-earning partnerships take a pride in their work and lifestyle. They get satisfaction from their work and want to be efficient, effective and productive in their professional lives. Some realise they need to put boundaries between their work and leisure times and create time for their hobbies and family needs.

Locus of Control

The locus of control is where we perceive the control centre of our lives to be located. Some people believe that they are in control of their lives and are masters of their own destiny. They believe they are not victims of circumstance and that they are in charge of their lives. They are in the driver's seat. They have an attitude of "I can make things happen" or "I am the captain of my ship and the master of my destiny". Even if you can't control the reality of a situation, you can choose your response or attitude to it. Some people develop a chronic dependency on others. They perpetually crave other people's approval.

Internal Locus of Control

People with an internal locus of control are happier, have better morale, and are more successful. They believe that good outcomes are due to their own efforts and bad outcomes due to external uncontrollable influences or bad luck. They know how to delay gratification and keep on target to achieve their goals. They have the tenacity and resilience to keep on going when life gets tough. They enjoy better health and recover more quickly from illness. They suffer less from anxiety and manage stress better. They enjoy better relationships and have higher self-esteem. They take responsibility for the failures, mistakes as well as the successes in their lives. They are in charge of their own thinking and make their own choices and take their own actions.

People with an internal locus of control believe in the law of cause and effect. This is what is meant by sayings like "You reap what you sow"; "You make your bed and lie in it"; and "What goes around comes around". Thoughts cause actions; actions have effects. There is no doubt that we are responsible for the state of our own lives. To change your life you've got to change the causes or actions that you are currently carrying out. To get different results you must take different actions. Keep on doing the same old thing and you surely will get the same old results.

External Locus of Control

People with an external locus of control believe that external forces determine the direction of their lives. They believe bad outcomes are their own fault and that positive happenings are due to good luck. They believe they are pawns of fate. Thus they abdicate responsibility for their actions and adopt a victim mentality, blaming others and circumstances for their plight. They wait for other people to do things for them and accept little personal accountability.

If you spend your time waiting for other people to take charge of your life or career you are going to be sorely disappointed. People have their own interests at heart rather than yours. People with an external locus of control are totally devoid of initiative and thus plod their way through life. They moan and groan but do nothing to change their circumstances. Their plight is caused by everybody but themselves — the government, the boss, fate, luck, astrology, circumstances, inheritance and parents.

Importance of Internal Control

If you want to be a success in life you need to adopt an internal locus of control. Your aim should be to make things happen and so determine your own future. A person once said that there were three types of people: those who make things happen, those who watch things happen, and those who haven't a clue what's happening. You will want to be in the first category.

Having an internal focus of control makes you feel good about yourself and can also improve your health and morale. Myers (1992) reports that having a strong sense of controlling one's life is a more dependable predictor of positive feelings of well-being than any other objective conditions of life. One study by Yale psychologist Judith Rodin encouraged nursing home patients to exert more control — to make choices about their environment and to influence policy. As a result, 93 per cent became more alert, active and happy. Similar results have been observed after allowing prisoners to move chairs and control the lights and TV.

The Comfort Zone

Most of us are stuck in a rut. In psychology this is called the comfort zone. We feel comfortable doing the things we have always done and are reluctant to do something different. We become comfortable in a particular job or relationship and are afraid to make changes, even for the better. We take the same route to work, eat the same food and go away on holidays with the same people to the same destination. Anything different or untried lies outside the comfort zone and is thus shunned. We choose the path of safety rather than the path of risk. We lack the confidence to leave our comfort zone and experience the discomfort of change. We fear change and don't realise that most of our fears never materialise. We never consider what is the worst thing that could possibly happen if we decide to do what we want to do.

Personal development, growth and self-actualisation come from venturing beyond and expanding our comfort zone. People who don't ever venture outside their comfort zone never realise their dreams or achieve their goals. People who succeed in life are prepared to take risks.

"I could say that I am terribly frightened and fear is terrible and awful and it makes me uncomfortable. Or I could say get used to being uncomfortable doing something that's risky. But so what? Do you want to stagnate and just be comfortable?" — Barbra Streisand

The Comfort Zone Model

Malone (1999) illustrates the difference between the comfort zone, the stretch zone, the strain zone and the panic zone. Your objective should be to move smoothly from the comfort zone, where you are underachieving, to the stretch zone, where you fulfil your true potential. This is attained by being committed to the task, not being afraid to take appropriate risk, while at the same time having a balanced approach to work and recreation. On the journey from the comfort zone to the stretch zone it is important not to get side-tracked into the panic or strain zone.

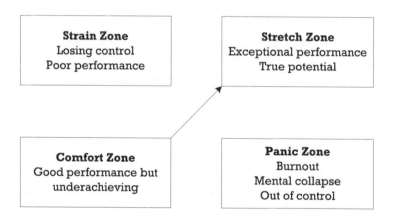

The Comfort Zone

This is where you feel most comfortable. It offers you challenge and stimulation without being overstretched. You are not under pressure and feel comfortable with your life. You won't get ulcers in the comfort zone but neither will you do anything exceptional. You need challenges from time to time to keep you on your toes. You can expand your comfort zone by the use of creative imagination and mental imagery or visualisation. Practise in your mind through mental rehearsal the new beliefs that you want to adopt. This will prepare your mind to get used to the idea of the new comfort zone.

The Stretch Zone

This is the zone which takes you out of your comfort zone. It offers challenge and you begin to feel under pressure. Acknowledge the fear and do it anyway. In order to move out of the comfort zone and into the stretch zone you must convert fear into excitement and enthusiasm. One way of doing this is to bombard your subconscious with positive thoughts and images through the use of affirmations and visualisations. This will prepare your mind for the challenges to come. It is only through stretching and testing yourself that you will grow and develop. Take the next step towards your goal. In this zone you will learn more, acquire new skills, increase your self-esteem and self-confidence and equip yourself to take on even more challenges. In the stretch zone you have the energy and confidence to keep going. This is the zone you're in when taking risks and undertaking new challenges. Sometimes it is called the "flow" zone (see previous chapter).

The Strain Zone

Here you are overstretched and losing control. Life is no longer giving you satisfaction and your performance and health deteriorate. You begin to experience a lot of stress. You need to nip the problem in the bud before it gets out of control by putting balance and fun back into your life. Moving too far outside your comfort zone results in decreased effectiveness and poor performance. Take time out for rest, recreation, recuperation and relaxation.

The Panic Zone

Here you are stressed out and feel you can't cope. Something snaps and you feel overwhelmed. You are easily irritated and argumentative. Your colleagues may notice this decline but you may be completely unaware of it yourself. These are the symptoms of a pending nervous breakdown. Some executives drive themselves into this state through excessive work and may finish up in a complete state of burnout and mental collapse.

Control Your Time

Successful people know how to get the best results out of the time they have. They know that time is the most precious resource they have and are thus reluctant to waste it. They realise that being busy is not the same as being effective.

"Activities are inclined to expand in line with the amount of time available for their completion." — Parkinson's Law
---

Thus we are inclined to waste valuable time. The following are some tips to help you achieve more in less time:

- Plan each week and plan each day. Begin each day with a list of tomorrow's priorities. Complete high priority tasks before you attempt the low priority ones. Plan and schedule your work. Strike items on your to-do list as the day proceeds. This will give you a feeling of accomplishment. Some people find it useful to start on the most unpleasant task in order to get it out of the way.

- Do one thing at a time. Clear any clutter from your desk. Concentrate on the most important tasks first and progressively work down through the priorities on your to-do list.

- Avoid unnecessary meetings and set time limits for those you attend. Do you really need to stay for the entire meeting even when the item concerning you has been dealt with?

- Bin junk mail. Unnecessary handling or reading such mail is a waste of time.

- Handle each piece of paper only once.

- Avoid procrastination and take control of your time. Never put off until tomorrow what you can do today unless there are very good reasons for doing so. People procrastinate because they fear failure, the task is too big or difficult, or the task is not important enough on their list of priorities. Ways of eliminating procrastination include visualising the end result, chunking, clearing the clutter out of the way, and operating to a to-do list. Chunking is also known as the SWAP approach — "start with a part".

"Whatever you do, or dream you can, begin it. Boldness has genius, power and magic in it. Begin it now."
— Goethe

- Eliminate wasteful activities and needless interruptions. Interruptions prevent us from maintaining our momentum. As Newton said: "A body at rest tends to remain at rest, while a body in motion tends to remain in motion". The most important aspect of doing anything is starting it and sticking to it until it is finished. Interruptions bring you to a halt and interfere with your sense of momentum and line of concentration. So do everything possible to remove yourself from the source of interruptions.

- Work smarter, not harder, by developing efficient methods of work. There are always better ways of doing anything. It is your job to develop efficient methods for your routines. Develop good filing and retrieval systems. This prevents wasting time trying to find things when you need them. Learn computer skills and use them to take over jobs that can be done more efficiently by the computer.

- Learn to speed read and read only essential material. The average reader reads at a speed of 240 words a minute. This can be improved with a little training to a speed of 360 words per minute, which is an improvement of 50 per cent. With sustained effort and plenty of practice you can improve on this considerably without loss of comprehension. Doing a speed-reading course is probably one of the best ways of improving your personal productivity and may be one of the best investments of your life.

- Chunk activities so that you do similar activities together and thus benefit from economies of scale. Thus you could chunk the phone calls you make to a particular time of day or complete the filing all in one go.

- Keep the Pareto Principle in mind — 80 per cent of your success is due to 20 per cent of what you do. Concentrate on the 20 per cent for greater effectiveness.

- Consider the best time of day for doing difficult work. Some people are "early birds" and do their best work in the morning. Others are "owls" and do their best work in the afternoon or evening. Always plan your most difficult tasks when your are at your best. Harness your physical and creative energy when it's at its peak.

- Avoid perfectionism. Work to your best standards but don't aim for 100 per cent perfection. Perfectionism wastes time. Perfectionists avoid starting a task because they fear that they might fall short of their own high standards. Perfectionists are reluctant to delegate as they believe that nobody can do the work as good as they can.

- Delegate appropriate work to others that can do it just as well. If you don't delegate work you will find yourself overloaded and under increased stress. Delegate both at home and at work. Parents can teach their children responsibility by delegating important but feasible tasks for them to do. If necessary you may have to give people some instruction or training to take over your tasks. This may be time-consuming in the short term but will pay dividends in the long term by freeing you up to pay attention to more important tasks. You are also developing people by giving them more responsibility and more interesting work. You will need to plan effectively to delegate effectively.

- Have contingency plans. Remember Murphy's Law: anything that can go wrong will go wrong, and it will go wrong at the worst possible time. Your car can break down, computers can malfunction, printers can fail, and important papers can get misplaced. So you need to build extra time into any job you plan to do to provide for contingencies.

Control Your Money

The vast majority of people are not financially literate. Most people spend what they earn each week and many more spend more and get involved in credit. These people are living beyond their means. Some people don't control their finances and are unaware of what they have in the bank at any particular time. One of the greatest sources of disharmony and unhappiness in families usually is caused by money problems. Some of these problems could be avoided if people became more financially aware. The following are some basic tips to help you control your finances:

- Calculate your net worth. List all your assets and liabilities. Your assets would include items like your house, car, furniture, investments and so on. Put a value on these at what you would get for them if you sold them. Do the same with your liabilities. These would include mortgages, loans and other debts that you may have. Subtract your total liabilities from your total assets. This is your net worth. If this amount is negative, it means that you are living beyond your means and should take immediate action to rectify the situation. Your objective should be to create assets rather than incur liabilities.

- Calculate your income and expenditure. This should be done on a monthly basis. Your income would include your salary, interest received and any other sources of income. Your expenditure would include mortgage repayments or rent, upkeep and maintenance of your home, car repayments and running costs, food costs, electricity, heating, insurance, phone, postage and so on. Subtract your expenditure from your income and the result will be a surplus or a deficit. If the result is a deficit you should review your expenditure and cut back on non-essentials. If you are lucky to have a surplus you can increase your savings.

- Credit cards. Consider getting rid of your credit cards. They are convenient but contribute to the "spend, spend, spend" mentality. A debit or laser card could be substituted for them, which means that you must have money in the bank before you can spend. Credit cards attract substantial interest charges if the credit terms are exceeded. Paying by cash will make you more aware of the value of money and how much you can spend. If you haven't the money, you must do without. It forces you to live within your means, buying the things you really need rather than the things that you want and can't afford. Generally, it should be your aim to save for the things that you can't afford immediately rather than funding them through loans and incurring debt and interest charges. Money matters are one of the chief sources of stress. You can eliminate this problem by practising financial discipline.

- Save a proportion of your earnings. It is a good idea to save about 10 per cent of your income. Don't touch this money but leave it on deposit to grow with compound interest. You may need a reserve if hard times come your way. In the future, poor health, redundancy, divorce and so on may drain your financial resources. It is times like these that you will appreciate the fact that you have put money away for such contingencies. In addition you should subscribe to a retirement plan from an early age. Remember, the state pension will only provide you with a very meagre existence.

Summary

Self-discipline will let you live a successful and satisfying life. So many people ruin their lives through relationship and money management problems. Successful people have a high level of emotional maturity, introspection and social skills. Being in control of your emotions means you can postpone the desire for instant gratification and stifle impulsive behaviour.

Many people are overwhelmed by the constant pressure of their work and desire a happier and more balanced lifestyle. They want to have more leisure time and time for their families.

Some are even prepared to take a job with a lower status and salary but more time off to achieve their goal.

"Because you are in control of your life. Don't ever forget that. You are what you are because of the conscious and subconscious choices you have made." — Barbara Hall

---

People with an internal locus of control are more in control of their lives and are happier and more successful. They are masters of their own fate. On the other hand, people with an external locus of control believe that external forces determine the direction of their lives. They abdicate responsibility for their lives to others and adopt a victim attitude blaming other people and circumstances for their problems and failures.

Most of us are stuck in a rut and are afraid to move out of our comfort zone. We become comfortable with a particular lifestyle and are afraid to make changes, even for the better. Unless we move from the comfort zone into the stretch zone we will never achieve much.

One way of controlling our lives is by taking control of our time. Successful people don't waste time. They realise that time is the most precious resource they have and thus they practise good time management skills. Money problems are a major source of stress. You should practise basic financial discipline and eliminate this source of stress from your life.

FIVE STEPS TO IMPROVE CONTROL

1. Bite your lip or count to ten the next time you are confronted with someone who says something that you find irritating, annoying or stupid.

2. Draw up a plan for work–life balance and take steps to implement it.

3. Reflect on where your locus of control lies. Adopt an internal locus of control to take charge of your life.

4. Occasionally do something to take you out of your comfort zone. Take up new hobbies, develop new skills, make new friends and go to different holiday destinations.

5. Draw up a short-term and long-term personal financial plan. The short-term plan should itemise your weekly income and expenditure over the next month. Your long-term plans should itemise your monthly income and expenditure over the next twelve months. Consider ways in which you could reduce your expenditure or indeed increase your income.

Case Study: Work–Life Balance

John and Mary are a young married couple with two children. They are both pursuing successful careers as accountants. They have two young children. They live in Kildare about 35 miles outside Dublin and commute each day to work. With traffic congestion the commute often takes up to 90 minutes each way. This means they are spending 15 hours in the car each week. House prices in Dublin are so expensive that they could not afford a house in Dublin.

They leave their children at a crèche each morning at 7.00 am before they start their commute to Dublin. They are back in Kildare around 7.00 pm to collect the children from the crèche. Consider what they have to do each day and the stress involved. They wake the children up, get them washed, dressed and fed, and then take them to the crèche. They then commute to work, work an eight-hour day, travel home from work and pick up their children. They help them with their homework, cook dinner, share quality time, put them to bed and then start the same process the next morning again. It's not surprising that they are feeling stressed. They also realise that they are not spending enough quality time with their family.

Mary in the past has considered leaving her job but now considers that it is not an option. She feels that the benefits of working outweigh the costs. She enjoys the independent identity that work provides, the job satisfaction, the increased self-esteem and the social contacts. In addition, they need the money to pay their big mortgage and support a comfortable lifestyle.

Recently they have begun to question the type of lifestyle they are living and are actively considering alternatives. They have come to the conclusion that they should be putting their family happiness before work. Work should be a means to an end and not an end in itself. They are prepared to sacrifice career advancement and make career changes to keep the family as the number one priority in their life. They realise that a joint income is necessary to pay the mortgage and pay for the childminding expenses. They examined the various types of flexible working hours available, such as part-time working, job-sharing, flexitime, annualised hours, term-time working, compressed working week, reduced working hours and home working. Mary decided that home working might be the best option for them if the company she worked for would consider the idea. Unlike John, she finds the option of having more time with the children attractive. Besides, John earns more money than she does.

Mary approached the Human Resource Manager in the company and raised the possibility of home working with him. The Human Resource Manager believed that employees who are helped to live balanced lives make better employees in the long run. The company had a policy of facilitating staff with flexible working arrangement if at all feasible. He listened very sympathetically to her case. After much consideration of the various alternatives they came to an arrangement whereby Mary would work a four-day week, working three days from home and one day in the office. She would have every Friday free. However, she agreed to take a small cut in salary for this arrangement. The company offered to equip one of her rooms and convert it into an office. With modern technology and the internet it is now feasible to work effectively from home.

The new arrangements have made a huge difference to their domestic lives. Mary now drops the kids off at the crèche at 9.00 am three mornings a week and then returns to her home to do her work. She collects the kids at 5.00 pm and brings them home. Every Friday she minds the kids herself and finds the experience very rewarding and fulfilling. She finds that she can work more effectively from home and because there are no interruptions her productivity has increased significantly. In fact she is able to do five days' work in four and the company are very satisfied with the way the arrangement has worked out. It has proved to be a win-win situation for everybody involved. She also has more time for the kids and feels more relaxed when John comes home. She feels that she has greater control over how she plans and does her work. The company has gained through her greater productivity. She hasn't lost out financially when the reduction in childminding charges are taken into account. The stress and strain has gone out of the marriage and they now have more time to enjoy each other's company. Mary now finds that she can balance work and home responsibilities better and in addition has more quality time with the family.

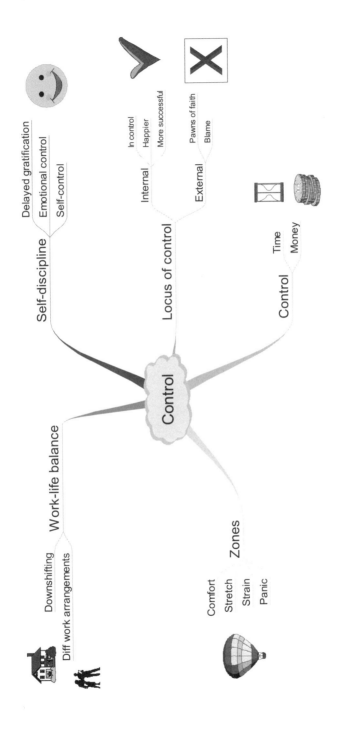

Control

Self-discipline
- Delayed gratification
- Emotional control
- Self-control

Locus of control
- Internal
  - In control
  - Happier
  - More successful
- External
  - Pawns of faith
  - Blame

Control
- Time
- Money

Work-life balance
- Downshifting
- Diff work arrangements

Zones
- Comfort
- Stretch
- Strain
- Panic

References and Bibliography

Agrawal, Manju and Dalal, Ajit K. (2001) "Beliefs About World and Recovery From Myocardial Infarction". *The Journal of Social Psychology*. Vol. 133(3). pp. 385-394.

Alexander, Amy (2004) Greater Baton Rouge Business Report. March 16, 2004.

Albrecht, Karl (2004) "Social Intelligence: Beyond IQ". *Training*. Dec 2004. Vol. 41, Issue 12, p. 26.

Austin, L. (2000) *What's Holding You Back?* New York: Basic Books.

Barth, Ariane (1993) "Pursuing the secret of happiness – physical and psychological aspects of happiness". *World Press Review*. April, 1993.

Bates, Tony (2005) "Resilient mental health". *Irish Times*, 11 October, 2005.

Baumeister, Roy F., Campbell, Jennifer D., Krueger, Joachim I. and Vohs, Kathleen D. (2003) "Does High Self-Esteem Cause Better Performance, Interpersonal Success, Happiness, or Healthier Lifestyles?" *Psychological Science in the Public Interest*. American Psychological Society. Vol. 4. No. 1., May 2003.

Bauman, James (2000) "The Gold Medal". *Psychology Today*. May/June 2000.

Blum, Deborah. (1998) "Finding Strength, How to Overcome Anything". *Psychology Today*. May/June 1998.

Bower, B. (2001) "Look on the bright side and survive longer". *Science News*. 26 May 2001.

Brody, Jane E. (2005) "Get a Grip and Set Your Sights Above Adversity". *The New York Times*, 1 March 2005.

Brown, Walter A. (1997) "The Best Medicine?" *Psychology Today*. Sept/Oct 1997.

Bruce, Barbara K. (1998) "Is it time for an attitude adjustment? Avoiding chronic depression and anxiety — includes related information on positive thinking". *USA Today* (Society for the Advancement of Education). Sept. 1998.

Burke, Jason (2001) "Confident kids likely to try drugs." Society-Guardian.co.uk. Sunday, 11 February 2001.

Carducci, Bernado J. and Zimbardo, Philip G. (1995). "Are You Shy?" *Psychology Today*. Nov/Dec 1995.

Carlin, Flora (2005) "The Measuring Game: Why You Think You'll Never Stack Up". *Psychology Today*. October 2005. Vol. 38. Issue 5. pp. 42-50.

Carlin, Flora (2005) "Happy hour". *Psychology Today*, Jan-Feb 2005.

Carlowe, Jo (2004) "Do you feel lucky?" *Guardian*, Sunday, 18 April 2004.

Colvin, Richard (2000) "Losing Faith in Self-Esteem — instilling positive feelings for better academic achievement". *School Administrator*. February 2000.

Coover, G and Murphy, C. (2000) "The Communicated Self: Exploring the Interaction between Self and Social Context". *Human Communication Research*, Vol. 26. pp. 125-47.

Csikszentmihalyi, Mihaly (1991) *The Psychology of Optimal Experience*. New York, HarperCollins.

Diener, E. and Fujita. F. (1995) "Resources, Personal Strivings, and Subjective Well-Being". *Journal of Personality and Social Psychology*. Vol. 68. p. 653.

Doheny, Kathleen (2004) "The limits of self-esteem". *Shape*. October 2004.

Frank, Robert H. (2004) "How not to buy happiness". *Daedalus*. Spring 2004.

Glass, J.C. and Jolly, G. (1997) "Satisfaction in Later Life". *Educational Gerontology*. Vol. 23. pp. 297.

Goode, Stephen (2000) "There's Power in Positive Thinking – study shows optimists live longer". *Psychology Today*. 13 March 2000.

Goldstein, Naomi (2001) "Positive Thinking – success of cancer treatment and positive outlook of patient". *Psychology Today*, July 2001.

Groskop, Viv (2004) "Psychology: time to deflate the bloated egos". *New Statesman*, 11 October 2004.

Honigsbaum, Mark (2004) "On the happy trail". *Observer*, Sunday, 4 April 2004.

Johnson, Catherine (2000) "Promised land or purgatory? Whether old age is worth living depends largely on mental health." *Scientific American 2000*.

Jourdan, Thea (2005) "Walking, riding, fishing — or just looking at the countryside — can boost people's self-esteem, according to new research". *Daily Telegraph*. 21 March 2005.

Katz, Stan J. and Liu, Aimee E. (1992) "Success in the land of less". *Psychology Today*. January/February 1992.

Kimble, Charles E, Kimble, Emily A. and Croy, Nan. A. (1998) "Development of Self-Handicapping Tendencies". *The Journal of Social Psychology*, Vol. 138(4), pp. 524-534.

Kornet, Allison (1997) "The Truth about Lying". *Psychology Today*. May/June 1997.

Lawson, Willow (2005) "Good Friends, Long Life". *Psychology Today*. Sept/Oct 2005.

Layard, Richard (2003) "The secrets of happiness: Despite growing affluence, the average Briton is more miserable than ever". *New Statesman*, 3 March 2003.

Leavy, Walter (2002) "Facing the fear of failure — For Brothers Only". *Ebony*. Sept. 2005.

Malone, Samuel A. (1999) *Success Skills for Managers*. Dublin: Oak Tree Press.

Marano, Hara Estroff. (1994) "Let us now praise ordinary pleasures — keys to happiness". *Psychology Today*. July/August 1994.

McLeod, Beverly (1986) "Rx for health: a dose of self-confidence; the mind can help the body mend when you learn to cope with what you fear". *Psychology Today*. Oct 1986.

Murray, C. and Peacock, M.J. (1996) "A Model-Free Approach to the Study of Subjective Well-Being". *Mental Health in Black America*. Thousand Oaks, CA: Sage.

Myers, David G. (1992). "The secrets of happiness — excerpts from *The Pursuit of Happiness: Who is Happy and Why?*" *Psychology Today*. July/August 1992.

Peterson, R., Cannito, M., and Brown, S. (1995). "An explanatory investigation of voice characteristics and selling effectiveness". *Journal of Personal Selling and Sales Management*. Vol. 15. pp. 1-15.

Rooney, James J. and Hopen, Deborah (2004). "What's In? What's Out? Defining your Problem: About Happiness". *The Journal of Quality and Participation*. Winter 2004.

Reeves, Richard (2004) "Friendship is the invisible thread running through society". *New Statesman*, 19 April 2004.

Scarnati, James T. (1998) "Beyond technical competence: a passion for persistence". *Career Development International*, Vol. 3. No. 1. pp. 23-25.

Science News (2003) "Findings puncture self-esteem claims", 7 June 2003.

Sherer, M (1996) "The Impact of Using Personal Computers on the Lives of Nursing Home Residents". *Physical and Occupational Therapy in Geriatrics*. Vol. 14. p. 13.

Solomon, J. (1996) "Humour and Ageing Well". *American Behaviour Scientist*. Vol. 39. p. 249.

Synder, C.R. (2002) "Hope Theory: Rainbows in the Mind". *Psychological Inquiry*. Vol. 13. No. 4. pp. 249-275.

Toynbee, Polly (2001). "At last we can abandon that tosh about low self-esteem". *Guardian*, 28 December 2001.

Vibrant Life (2002) "Don't worry, live longer — Lifelines". Sept-Oct 2002.

INDEX

ABCDE technique, 135, 155–7
A Brief History of Time, 73
Adams, Arthur S., 55
Adams, John Quincy, 44
Albrecht, Karl, 92
Alcoholics Anonymous, 44
Alexander, Amy, 101
Anderson, Greg, 69
Armstrong, Lance, 48
Ash, Mary Kay, 64
ASPIRE model, 25–7
assertiveness, 98–9
  basic skills, 100–1
    "ALL technique", 101
    "broken record", 100
    "fogging", 101
    saying "no", 100
Augustine, Norman R., 82

Bannister, Roger, 75, 137
Baran, Paul, 39
Bates, Tony, 45
Baudouin, Charles, 118
Baumeister, Roy F., 120, 124
Bill of Rights, My, 99–100
Bittel, Lester R., 25
Blum, Deborah, 45
Boesky, Ivan, 62
Borge, Victor, 96
Bower, Sharon, Anthony, 98

brain, *see* learning
Branden, Nathaniel, 112, 116
Brody, Jane, 46, 47
Brooks, Dr Robert, 46
Brown, Ernestine, 46
Brown, Walter A., 77
Buddha, 139, 151
Butler, Edward B., 80

Cabell, James Branch, 139
Carlin, Flora, 71
Carnegie, Dale, 39, 104
Chandler, Steve, 155
change, 164–6
  stages, 164–5
character, 56–7
Character Creed, The, 60
Churchill, Winston, 59, 135
Clinton, Bill, 61
Collier, Jeremy, 74
comfort zone, 189–92
  model, 190
commitment, 36–7
communication skills, 93–4
control, 183–200
  locus of, 187–9
    external, 188
    internal, 187–8, 189
  money and, 195–6
  time and, 192–5

Coolidge, Calvin, 35
Coward, Noel, 37
Creasey, John, 41
Csikszentmihalyi, Mihalyi, 176–7
Curie, Marie, 17

D'Angelo, Anthony J., 169
da Vinci, Leonardo, 9, 12
Danner, Deborah, 139
Dawson, George, 47
Disney, Walt, 12
Dyer, Wayne, 72

Edison, Thomas Alva, 38, 137
Edmunds, J. Ollie, 73
Einstein, Albert, 12, 57
Eliot, George, 9
Emerson, Ralph Waldo, 70
Emler, Professor, 122–3
expectation, 75–6
Epicurus, 145

FARSIGHTED, 142–4
Fermat's Last Theorem, 40
flow zone, 176–7, 191
Ford, Henry, 78
Fox, Tery, 49
Franklin, Benjamin, 146
Freud, Sigmund, 80

Gallozzi, Chuck, 166
Gandhi, Mahatma, 36, 115, 129
Gardner, Howard, 170
Gates, Bill, 42, 78
Gelb, Michael J., 4
goals, 4–18
   basic questions for, 14–16
   importance of, 4–5
   need for multiple, 13
   stretch, 5–6
   types of, 11–3
   why people don't set, 8–11
   written, 5
Goethe, 193

Gold, Ron, 140
Goldstein, Dr Sam, 46
Gracian, Baltasar, 62

Hall, Barbara, 197
happiness, 145–50
   habituation and, 148
   health and, 150
   J-curve and, 146–7
   little things and, 146
   money and, 147–8
   practical steps towards, 150–5
   relative deprivation and, 149
Harpham, Dr Wendy Schlessel,
   47
Hart, Louise, 124
Hawking, Stephen, 73
Hazlitt, Henry, 79
Heilein, Robert, 6
Hemingway, Ernest, 95
Hilary, Sir Edmund, 36, 137
Hildebrand, Kenneth, 75
Hill, Dr Napoleon, 75
Holmes, Oliver Wendell, 10
hope, 72–5
Horner, Martina, 170
How to Think Like Leonardo da
   Vinci, 4
Hunt, Leigh, 152
Huxley, Thomas Henry, 41

improvement, 163–80
integrity, 55–66
interpersonal relationships, 89–
   108

James, William, 145
Johnson, Lady Bird, 103
Johnson, Samuel, 42, 175
Jung, Carl, 174

Katz, Stan J., 13
Keller, Helen, 58
Kennedy, John F., 136

King, Martin Luther, 79
KISS, 96
Kubler-Ross, Elisabeth, 165

"Ladder of St Augustine", 48
Lakein, Alan, 27
Land, Dr Edward, 78
learned helplessness, 119
learning, 166–76
  ageing and, 173–6
  brain and, 167–9
  cycle, 171
  effective, 171–2
  lifelong, 166–7
Leavy, Walter, 47
Leeson, Nick, 62
Liddon, H.P., 183
lies, 61–2
  business, 62
Life is So Good, 47
Lincoln, Abraham, 39
Lindbergh, Charles, 137
listening skills, 94–6
  avoid formal language, 95–6
  mirroring, 95, 97
Longfellow, Henry Wadsworth, 48
Lowell, Albert L., 163

MacArthur, Mary Hardy, 111
Macaulay, Thomas B., 59
Maltz, Maxwell, 126
Mandela, Nelson, 38
Marconi, 9
Marden, Orison Swett, 47
Marston, Ralph, 45
Maslow, Abraham, 72, 113
May, Rollo, 94
McGuirk, John J., 89
Meyer, Paul, J., 4
Michelangelo, 17
Mill, John Stuart, 145
Mother Teresa, 11, 79

motivation, 69–86
  unique drivers of, 71–2
Mozart, Wolfgang Amadeus, 12
multiple intelligence, 169–71
Murphy's Law, 194
musturbation, 126

narcissism, 120–1
Nelson, Donald M., 28
Newton, Sir Isaac, 57
Nixon, Richard, 61

objectives, 3–20
O'Dell, Tawni, 39
optimism
  unrealistic, 140
optimists, 137–9
  longevity of, 138
Ortega y Gasset, Jose, 11

Pareto Principle, 194
Parkinson's Law, 192
passion, 78–80
Pasteur, Louis, 37
patience, 40–1
Peale, Norman Vincent, 143, 156
Peary, Robert E., 17
persistence, 37–40
personal code of ethics, 55–6
Personal Development Plans (PDPs), 29–30
  drawing up, 30
pessimism
  dealing with, 140–2
pessimists, 139–42
Picasso, Pablo, 14
Placebo Effect, 77–8
planning, *see* plans
  barriers to, 27–8
  importance of, 24
plans, 23–32
popularity, 90–2

positive thinking, *see* thinking
   positively
Pretty, Jules, 114
Pushing to the Front, 47
Pygmalion Effect, 76–7

Reagan, Ronald, 92–3
Rector, Hartman Jr., 121
Reeve, Christopher, 72–3
Reeves, Richard, 102
Reiki Principles, 152–3
resilience, 43–8
resolutions, 42–3
Robbins, Tony, 12, 78
Rohn, Jim, 185
Rockefeller, John D., 153
Roosevelt, Eleanor, 127
Roosevelt, Franklin D., 148
Rusnak, John, 62

Salovey, Peter, 71
Santayana, George, 57
Schweitzer, Albert, 80, 145
Science News, 124
seasonal affective disorder
   (SAD), 141
self-control, *see* control
self-discipline, 184–5
self-efficacy, 117–9
self-esteem, 111–32
   dark side of, 121–4
   exercise and, 114–5
   high, 112–4
   how to raise, 127–9
   limits of, 120
   low, 124–5
   personal development and,
   116

self-sabotage, 125–6
self-talk, 115–6
self-worth, 117
Seneca, 29
Sevareid, Eric, 47
Shaw, George Bernard, 12
shyness, 102–5
   overcoming, 102–5
SIMPLE, 96
Singer, Isaac Bashevis, 141
SMARTS, 3, 7–8, 10, 18
Snyder, C.R., 74
social intelligence (SI), 92
stamina, 48–9
Stone, Arthur A., 146
Streisand, Barbra, 190
Success magazine, 47
Sugarman, Joseph, 61
SWOT, 25

tenacity, 35–52
thinking positively, 135–60
trust, 63–4
   destroying, 63
Twain, Mark, 90, 151

values, 57–8
Vibrant Life, 138

Waitley, Denis, 128
Watergate, 61
Webster, Noah, 17
Werner, Emmy, 45
Wiles, Andrew, 40
work–life balance, 186–7

ABOUT THE AUTHOR

Samuel Malone has many years' experience as a training consultant, training manager and lecturer. He has an M.Ed (in training and development) from the University of Sheffield and is a qualified Chartered Management Accountant. He is the author of seven books including *Mind Skills for Managers* (Gower), *Learning about Learning* (CIPD London) and *A Practical Guide to Learning in the Workplace* (The Liffey Press).

He lives in Dublin.